Be Concerned

WARREN W. WIERSBE

D1483612

ChariotVICTOR
PUBLISHING
A DIVISION OF COOK COMMUNICATIONS

Chariot Victor Publishing,
a division of Cook Communications, Colorado 80918.
Cook Communications, Paris, Ontario
Kingsway Communications, Eastbourne, England

Editors: Jerry Yamamoto, Barbara Williams
Design: Scott Rattray
Cover Photo: Tony Stone Worldwide
Personal and Group Study Guide: Sue Moroney
Production: Julianne Marotz

Library of Congress Cataloging-in-Publication Data

Wiersbe, Warren W.
  Be concerned / Warren W. Wiersbe.
    p. cm.
  Includes bibliographical references.
  ISBN 1-56476-590-3
    1. Bible. O.T. Minor Prophets—Criticism, interpretation, etc.
  2. Bible. O.T. Minor Prophets—Study and teaching. I. Title.
BS1560.W56   1996
224'.906—dc20   96-30201
                                                         CIP

7 8 9 10 Printing / Year 05 04 03

BE CONCERNED

CONTENTS

PREFACE

This is the second of three volumes on the Minor Prophets in the *BE* series, dealing with Amos, Obadiah, Micah, and Zephaniah. The first volume *Be Amazed* covers Hosea, Joel, Jonah, Nahum, Habakkuk, and Malachi; and the third volume *Be Heroic* will cover the post-exilic prophets—Haggai and Zechariah—along with the Book of Ezra.

The Minor Prophets may be "minor" in size, as compared with Isaiah, Jeremiah, and Ezekiel, but they certainly aren't "minor" in their message. These men dealt courageously with the sins of God's people, warning them that chastening judgments would come if the people didn't repent and turn to God. But they were also tenderhearted in their message of forgiveness and hope.

In the words of Paul, these prophets proclaimed "the goodness and severity of God" (Rom. 11:22), a balanced message that we need to hear today. In our "pluralistic society," some preachers and teachers try so hard to be "politically correct" that they end up with no message at all, while others fail to understand the mind-set of their hearers and fail to get through. The prophets made neither mistake; and we can learn from them how best to declare God's truth so that the message reaches the mind and heart of each listener and motivates the will.

Having heard these messages, we need to act upon them and obey what God tells us to do. The great need of the hour is for "the company of the concerned" to follow Christ and accomplish His will in this needy world. Will you be among them?

Warren W. Wiersbe

Amos in His Time

Amos ("burden bearer") was a herdsman and a cultivator of sycamore trees (Amos 1:1; 7:14) when the Lord called him to be a prophet. He lived in the village of Tekoa, about eleven miles from Jerusalem, during the reigns of Uzziah in Judah (790–740 B.C.) and Jeroboam II in the Northern Kingdom of Israel (793–753). Amos was a "layman," a humble farmer and shepherd who was not an official member of the Jewish religious or political establishment.

At this time, both Judah and Israel were enjoying prosperity and security. Luxury abounded (3:10-15; 6:1-6), and "religion" was popular. Israel flocked to the royal chapel at Bethel (4:4-5), and Judah celebrated the feasts enthusiastically (5:21-22), but the sins of both nations were eroding the religious and moral fiber of the people. Making money was more important than worshiping God (8:5); the rich exploited the poor, the judicial system was corrupt, and injustice flourished (5:11-15, 24; 8:4-6).

Amos declared God's judgment not only on the Gentile nations but also on Israel and Judah. It was a call to repent of "ritual religion" and seek the Lord sincerely. He warned the aristocrats that God would judge them for the way they were abusing the poor. In spite of the nations' peace and prosperity, Amos saw the end coming and warned the people to prepare to meet their God.

One of the key verses in Amos is 5:24—"But let justice roll on like a river, righteousness like a never-failing stream!" (NIV) a command the nations need to obey today.

A Suggested Outline of the Book of Amos

Key theme: A call for justice, a warning of judgments
Key verse: Amos: 5:24

I. Look around and see God's judgment—1–2
Eight nations judged
   1. Six Gentile nations condemned—1:1-2:3
   2. Judah condemned—2:4-5
   3. Israel condemned—2:6-16

II. Look within and see the corruption—3–6
Three sermons to the people of Israel
   1. Message #1: Israel's judgment certain—3:1-15
   2. Message #2: Israel's sins denounced—4:1-13
   3. Message #3: Israel's doom lamented—5:1–6:14

III. Look ahead and see the end coming—7–9
   1. Five visions of judgment—7:1–9:10
      (1) The locusts—7:1-3
      (2) The fire—7:4-6
      (3) The plumb line—7:7-9
      Historical interlude: Amos at Bethel—7:10-17
      (4) The basket of summer fruit—8:1-14
      (5) The ruined temple—9:1-10
   2. A vision of the glorious kingdom—9:11-15

The Lion Roars!

If the Prophet Amos were to come to our world today, he would probably feel very much at home; for he lived at a time such as ours when society was changing radically. Both Israel and Judah were at peace with their neighbors, which meant that their wealth and energy could be used for developing their nations instead of fighting their enemies. Both kingdoms were prosperous; their cities were expanding rapidly; and a new wealthy merchant class was developing in society. The two kingdoms were moving from an agricultural to a commercial society and experiencing both the benefits and problems that come with that change.

However, in spite of their material success, all was not well with God's chosen people. They were experiencing what the British poet Oliver Goldsmith wrote about back in 1770:

> Ill fares the land, to hast'ning ills a prey,
> Where wealth accumulates, and men decay . . . [1]

There were ills aplenty in *all* the lands of that day, the Gentile nations as well as the Jewish kingdoms of Israel and Judah; and Amos wasn't afraid to name them. He opened his book with a denunciation of the sins of six Gentile nations, and no doubt the people of Israel and Judah applauded his words. Nothing would make the Jews happier than to see the Lord judge the surrounding nations. But when Amos denounced Judah and Israel, that was a different story; and his popularity began to suffer at that point.

1. Judgment on the Gentile nations (Amos 1:2–2:3)[2]

God wanted to get the nations' attention, but people weren't listening. You'd think they could hear a lion roar or the thunder roll and know that danger was at hand. God was speaking ("thundering") from Jerusalem, for judgment always begins at the house of the Lord (1 Peter 4:17). He had sent drought to the land so that even fruitful Carmel was withering, but it didn't bring the people to their knees. So God called a common farmer to preach to His people and warn them. "A lion has roared! Who will not fear? The Lord God has spoken! Who can but prophesy?" (Amos 3:8, NKJV)

Eight times Amos used the phrase "for three transgressions and for four," a Jewish idiom that means "an indefinite number that has finally come to the end." God is long-suffering with sinners (2 Peter 3:9), but He marks what they do and His patience eventually runs out. To try God's patience is to tempt the Lord; and when we tempt the Lord, we invite judgment.

Syria (Amos 1:3-5). Damascus was the capital of Syria, one of the Jews' persistent enemies. Amos denounced the Syrians for their inhuman treatment of the Israelites who lived in Gilead, east of the Jordan River. They cruelly "threshed them" as though they were nothing but stalks of grain. God had called the Syrians to punish Israel (2 Kings 10:32-33; 13:1-9), but the Syrians had carried it too far.

The man who began his prayer with "Lord, no doubt You saw in the morning newspaper . . . " was stating a great truth in a clumsy way: God sees how the nations treat one another, and He responds appropriately. Benjamin Franklin said it well at the Constitutional Convention, "I have lived, Sir, a long time, and the longer I live, the more convincing proofs I see of this truth—*that God governs in the affairs of men.*"[3]

The phrase "I will send a fire" (Amos 1:4, 7, 10, 12, 14; 2:2, 5) means "I will send judgment"; for fire represents the holiness and judgment of God (Deut. 4:11, 24, 36; Heb. 12:29). Indeed, the Lord did judge Syria: The dynasty of King Hazael ended; his son Ben-Hadad was defeated; Damascus lost its power (business was done at the city gate, Amos 1:5); and "the house of Eden" (delight, paradise) became a ruin. King Josiah defeated Ben-Hadad three times (2 Kings 13:25), but it was the Assyrians who finally subdued Syria and took them into captivity.

Philistia (Amos 1:6-8). Gaza, Ashdod, Ashkelon, Gath, and Ekron were the five key Philistine cities (Josh. 13:5), and Amos denounced all of them for trading in human lives.[4] They raided Jewish villages and captured people to be sold as slaves. To add insult to injury, the Philistines sold these slaves to Israel's ancient enemy, the Edomites. Since Edom was descended from Esau, Jacob's brother, it was a case of brother enslaving brother. (God had something to say to Edom in Amos 1:11-12.)

Throughout the history of ancient Israel, slavery was practiced, but the Law of Moses clearly governed how the slaves were to be treated. The law that permitted slavery at the same time protected the slaves. However, it was one thing to put a prisoner of war to work and quite something else to kidnap innocent people and sell them like cattle. Neither Jesus nor the apostles openly denounced slavery, but they made it clear that all people are sinners whom God loves and that all saved people are one and equal in Christ (Gal. 3:26-29). It took centuries for the light of the Gospel to dispel the darkness and make slavery illegal, although there are still places in our world where people are abused and exploited.

God's judgment on Philistia came in the days of King Uzziah (2 Kings 18:7-8) and the Assyrian invaders under Sargon and the Babylonians under Nebuchadnezzar. The slave masters were themselves taken into exile and slavery.

Tyre (Amos 1:9-10). Amos has moved from Damascus in the northeast to the Philistine cities in the southwest, and now he sets his sights straight north on Phoenicia and its major city, Tyre.

During the reigns of David and Solomon, Israel had a warm relationship with the people of Tyre (1 Kings 5:1ff). Amos called it "the brotherly covenant" ("treaty of brotherhood," NIV), suggesting that the "covenant" was more than a treaty but involved a friendly partnership that went deeper than politics. Even if the peoples of different nations don't agree in their religious practices or their political structure, they can still treat one another like fellow human beings.

Tyre, however, committed the same sins as the Philistine cities by selling Jewish captives to the Edomites as slaves (Amos 1:6-8). When the Prophet Ezekiel gave his funeral dirge celebrating the fall of Tyre, he mentioned this grievous sin (Ezek. 27:13). But Tyre's sin was worse than that of Philistia because Tyre was violating a long-standing compact that was based on friendship and a mutual respect for humanity. Tyre was selling its friends as slaves!

Judgment came in 332 B.C. when Alexander the Great wiped Tyre off the face of the earth and left it a place for drying nets (26:5, 14). "Though the mills of God grind slowly/yet they grind exceeding small."[5] When Rudyard Kipling published his poem "Recessional" during Queen Victoria's "Diamond Jubilee" in 1897, he used Tyre as a warning to any people who rebel against the will of God and mistreat men and women created in the image of God.

Far-called our navies melt away—
On dune and headland sinks the fire—
Lo, all our pomp of yesterday—
Are one with Nineveh and Tyre!

Edom (Amos 1:11-12). The Edomites nursed a long-standing grudge against the Jews, perpetuating the ancient rivalry between Jacob and Esau, which began before the twin boys were born (Gen. 25:21-26). In His sovereign will, God had chosen the younger brother, Jacob, to receive the blessings of the birthright and the Abrahamic Covenant (Mal. 1:2-3; Rom. 9:6-13). Esau despised his spiritual heritage and willingly sold his birthright to Jacob (Gen. 25:29-34; Heb. 12:14-17); but because Jacob cheated him out of the patriarchal blessing (Gen. 27), Esau vowed to kill Jacob. Later they were briefly reconciled, but the enmity continued (33:1-17). As far as the biblical record is concerned, their final meeting was at a funeral, where they buried their father but did not bury their bitterness (35:27-29).

The Edomites wouldn't allow their Jewish cousins to pass through their land during Israel's march to Canaan (Num. 20:14-21). King Saul suppressed the Edomite army (1 Sam. 14:47), and David conquered them (2 Sam. 8:14), but in the days of King Jehoram, Edom revolted against Judah and won their freedom (2 Kings 8:16-22).

Amos condemned the Edomites for their persistent hatred of the Jews, which the prophet described as "raging anger and flaming fury" (Amos 1:11; see also NIV). We don't know when the Edomites aided the enemy by pursuing the Jews with the sword. It could have been during any one of the numerous times when enemies invaded the land. When the Babylonians attacked and captured Jerusalem, the Edomites assisted the enemy and gave vent to their anger (Obad. 10-14; see Ps. 137:7). You would think that brother would help brother in a time of need, but the Edomites "cast off all pity" (Amos 1:11) and acted like beasts instead of humans. The phrase "his anger did tear" (v. 11) uses a verb that describes ferocious beasts tearing their prey (Ps. 7:2; Gen. 37:32).

Teman and Bozrah were strong cities that today don't exist. The Edomites lived "in the clefts of the rock" and had their "nest among the stars" (Obad. 3-4), boasting that their fortresses were impregnable; but the Lord destroyed their nation so thoroughly that nothing is left today except ruins. When the Romans attacked Jerusalem in A.D. 70, they destroyed what was left of the Edomite (Idumean) people, and Edom was no more.

Ammon (Amos 1:13-15). The Ammonites and Moabites (2:1-3) were the descendants of Lot through his incestuous union with his daughters (Gen. 19:30-38). They were a ruthless people who were the avowed enemies of the Jews (Deut. 23:3-6; 1 Sam. 11:2; Neh. 2:10-19; Jer. 40:14; 41:5-7). In order to enlarge their land, they invaded Gilead; and not satisfied with attacking the men defending their homeland, the Ammonites killed women and unborn children (see 2 Kings 8:12; 15:16). To the Ammonites, land was more important than people, including defenseless women and innocent children. Such brutality shocks us, but is "modern warfare" any kinder?

Amos announced that a storm of judgment would come to the people of Ammon and that their capital city (Rabbah) would be destroyed. This took place when the Assyrians swept over the land in 734 B.C. Not only did Amos predict the destruction of their land, but so did Ezekiel (25:1-7). The chief god of Edom was Molech (Malcham, Milcom), which means "reigning one, king." Amos 1:15 could be translated, "Molech will go into exile," thus showing the inability of their god to save them.

Moab (Amos 2:1-3). Animosity between Moab and Israel began very early when the Moabites refused to give the Jews passage on the major highway (Deut. 23:3-4; Jud. 11:17). The king of Moab also hired Balaam to curse Israel (Num. 22–24), and then the Moabite women seduced the Jewish men to commit fornication and idolatry (Num. 25). During the period of the judges, Israel was subject to the Moabites for eighteen years (Jud. 3:12-30).

What was the sin of Moab? Disrespect for the dead and for royalty. We don't know which king's remains were subjected to this humiliation, but the deed disgraced the memory of the king and humiliated the people of Edom. How would Americans feel if somebody disinterred John F. Kennedy's body and mistreated it? Or what would the British people do if the body of a famous person were stolen from Westminster Abbey and publicly abused?

For the most part, society today shows respect for the dead, but ancient Eastern peoples protected their dead even more. Steeped in pagan superstition, they interred bodies carefully to insure the spirit's continued existence in the next world. Relatives of the deceased often inscribed frightful curses on the tombs, warning people to refrain from opening them.[6]

Amos announced that the king of Moab and his officials were all guilty and would be destroyed, along with their cities.[7] Moab was taken by the Assyrians, and the land eventually became the home of numerous nomadic tribes. The nation of Moab was no more. (For other prophecies of Moab's doom, see Isa. 15–16; Jer. 48; Ezek. 25:8-11; Zeph. 2:8-11.)

Before we listen to God's messages to Judah and Israel, we should pause to reflect on the messages we have just studied that were delivered to six Gentile nations. *God expected these Gentiles to listen to a Jewish prophet and heed what he said!* Though not under the Mosaic Law, these nations were responsible to God for what they did; and responsibility brings accountability. God sees what the nations do, and He judges them accordingly. World news from day to day may give the impression that evil leaders and violent subversive groups are getting away with terrible crimes, but God is still on the throne and will punish evildoers in His good time. It is God who controls the rise and fall of the nations (Acts 17:24-28), and His judgments are always just.

2. Judgment on the kingdom of Judah (Amos 2:4-5)

In his six messages, Amos had announced judgment to the nations surrounding Israel and Judah, starting with Syria in the northwest and ending with the trans-Jordanic nations of Ammon, Moab, and Edom. (There's probably a map of the divided kingdom in the back of your Bible.) As his fellow Jews heard these denunciations of the Gentiles, no doubt they applauded and wanted to hear more. But when Amos focused on Israel and Judah (his own land), that changed their attitude completely. The very idea of a Jewish prophet classifying God's chosen people with the Gentile "dogs"! "We know we aren't a perfect people," the people of Judah would argue, "but at least we worship the true and living God!"

Yes, the temple was filled with people bringing their sacrifices, but Judah was a nation given over to idolatry. "Their lies [idols] lead them astray, lies after which their fathers walked" (2:4, NKJV). They were wandering like lost animals and like drunken men. The Gentiles had sinned against conscience and the laws of brotherhood and humanity, but the Jews had despised and rejected the very laws of God, given to them by Moses. Theirs was the greater sin, for greater privilege always brings greater responsibility (Rom. 2:17–3:9).

God had frequently punished His people *in their land* by allowing various nations to attack and subdue them, but now He would punish them *out of their land.* The Babylonian army would destroy Jerusalem and take thousands of captives to Babylon where they would live in the midst of gross idolatry for seventy years. However, unlike the six Gentile nations

Amos had denounced, Judah would not be destroyed but would be spared. In His mercy, God would allow a remnant of Jews to return to establish the nation and rebuild the temple.

"I don't know why you preach about the sins of Christians," a church member said to the pastor. "After all, the sins of Christians are different from the sins of unsaved people."

"Yes," replied the pastor, *"they're worse!"*

3. Judgment on the kingdom of Israel (Amos 2:6-16)

Both Israel and Judah were enjoying peace and prosperity, and divine judgment was the furthest thing from their minds. Remember, Jewish theology equated prosperity with God's blessing;[8] and as long as the people were enjoying "the good life," they were sure God was pleased with them. They knew what the Law said about their sins, but they chose to ignore the warnings.

Amos first exposes *their sinful present* and names three flagrant sins. To begin with, the people of the Northern Kingdom were guilty of *injustice (Amos 2:6-7a)*. Supported by corrupt judges, the rich were suing the poor, who couldn't pay their bills, and forcing them into servitude and slavery. Even if they couldn't pay for a pair of shoes, the poor were neither forgiven nor assisted. Instead, they were trampled like the dust of the earth. As we shall see in our continued studies, the Prophet Amos has a great deal to say about caring for the poor (see 4:1; 5:11; 8:6; also Deut. 15:7-11; Ex. 23:6-9; Prov. 14:31; 17:15).

Their second gross sin was *immorality (Amos 2:7b)*, with fathers and sons visiting the same prostitute! These may have been "cult prostitutes" who were a part of the heathen idolatrous worship. Thus there was a double sin involved: immorality *and* idolatry. Or the girl may have been a household servant or a common prostitute. You would think that a father would want to be a better example to his son by obeying the Law of Moses (Ex. 22:16; Deut. 22:28-29; 23:17-18). Perhaps what's described here is a form of incest, which was, of course, strictly forbidden by Moses (Lev. 18:7-8, 15; 20:11-12). Regardless of what the act of disobedience was, it was rebellion against God and defiled His holy name.

The third sin was *open idolatry (Amos 2:8).* The wealthy men took their debtors' garments as pledges but did not return them at sundown as the law commanded (Ex. 22:26-27; Deut. 24:10-13, 17). Instead, these rich sinners visited pagan altars, where they got drunk on wine purchased with the fines they exacted from the poor. Then, in their drunken stupor, they slept by the altars on other people's garments, defiling the garments and disobeying the law. The officials were getting rich by exploiting the people, and then were using their unjust gain for committing sin.

After describing their sinful present, Amos reminded them of *their glorious past (Amos 2:9-12).* God had led His people out of Egypt (v. 10a), cared for them in the wilderness (v. 10b), and destroyed other nations so the Jews could claim their inheritance in Canaan (vv. 9, 10c). He gave them His Word through chosen prophets (v. 11a), and He raised up dedicated people like the Nazirites (Num. 6) to be examples of devotion to God. What a glorious past they had! But instead of being humbled by these blessings, the people rebelled against the Lord by rejecting the messages of the prophets and forcing the Nazirites to break their holy vows. The Jews wanted neither the Word of God nor examples of godly living.

Amos closed his message with the announcement of *their terrible future (Amos 2:13-16).* Israel would be crushed by their own sins just as a loaded cart crushes whatever it rolls over. Judgment is coming, and nobody will be able to escape. The swift won't be able to run away; the strong won't be able to defend themselves; the armed will be as if unarmed; and even the horsemen will be unable to flee. The bravest soldiers will run away while shedding their equipment and clothing so they can run faster. Yes, Assyria would invade Israel (720 B.C.) and the nation would be no more.

Amos has looked around with eyes gifted with prophetic insight, and he has seen and announced what God would do to six Gentile nations and to the kingdoms of Judah and Israel. The lion has roared! Next, the prophet will *look within* and expose the corruption in the hearts of the Jewish people by explaining four divine calls.

But before we examine these four calls, we need to pause and ask ourselves whether we truly fear God and seek to obey His will. Just because we enjoy a measure of peace and prosperity, it doesn't mean God is pleased with us. For that matter, the goodness of God ought to lead us to repentance, as it did the Prodigal Son (Luke 15:17; Rom. 2:4).

"'Vengeance is Mine; I will repay,' says the Lord. And again, 'The Lord will judge His people.' It is a fearful thing to fall into the hands of the living God" (Heb. 10:30-31, NKJV).

However, we can still claim the promises of 2 Chronicles 7:14 and 1 John 1:9 and experience the forgiveness of the Lord.

Listen to What God Says

Now that Amos had the attention of the people, he proceeded to deliver three messages, each of which begins with "Hear this word" (3:1; 4:1; 5:1). By using this phrase, he reminded them that they weren't listening to a mere man making a speech; they were listening to a prophet declaring the living Word of God.

It's indeed a great privilege to have God speak to us, but it's also a great responsibility. If we don't open our hearts to hear His Word and obey Him, we're in grave danger of hardening our hearts and incurring the wrath of God. "Today, if you will hear His voice, do not harden your hearts" (Heb. 3:7-8; see Ps. 95:7-11, NKJV).

The first message (Amos 3:1-15) was one of *explanation*, in which Amos clarified four divine calls and announced that Israel's judgment was certain. His second message (4:1-13) focused on *accusation* in which the prophet denounced Israel's sins. The final message (5:1–6:14) was a *lamentation* as the prophet felt the anguish of his nation's certain doom.

In this first message, Amos explains the significance of four divine calls.

1. God called Israel (Amos 3:1-2)

This message was delivered to "the whole family," that is, to both Israel and Judah; for both kingdoms were guilty of disobeying God's holy Law. Amos reminded them of their divine calling as the people of God, a calling that they were prone to despise and forget.

What kind of a calling did God give to the Jewish nation? To begin with, it was a *gracious call;* for the Lord had chosen them and no other nation to be the special recipients of His bountiful gifts. "For you are a holy people to the Lord your God; the Lord your God has chosen you to be a people for Himself, a special treasure above all the peoples on the face of the earth. The Lord did not set His love on you nor choose you because you were more in number than any other people, for you were the least of all peoples; but because the Lord loves you, and because He would keep the oath which He swore to your fathers" (Deut. 7:6-8, NKJV; see Ex. 19:1-5).

This principle of gracious election also applies to the church. Jesus said, "You did not choose Me, but I chose you" (John 15:16, NIV); and Paul reminded the Corinthian believers that "not many wise men after the flesh, not many mighty, not many noble, are called"; but that God chose the foolish, the weak, the base, and the despised "that no flesh should glory in his presence" (1 Cor. 1:26, 29). God chose us in Christ before the foundation of the world (Eph. 1:4), and it was purely an act of grace.

God's call was also an *effective call (Amos 3:1b),* for the Lord had demonstrated His great power in delivering Israel from the bondage of Egypt. The blood of the lamb protected the Jews from death, and they were taken through the Red Sea to be separated from Egypt forever. Christians today have been saved by the precious blood of Christ (1 Peter 1:18-19; 2:24) and separated from the world because of His mighty resurrection (Eph. 1:19-23).

Third, their calling was an *exclusive call (Amos 3:2a)*. "You only have I chosen [*known,* KJV] of all the families of the earth" (NIV). The word "known" indicates an intimate relationship, such as that of husband and wife (Gen. 4:1). "To know" means "to choose" (see 18:19; Jer. 1:5; 2:2-3), a term Paul applies to Christian believers (Rom. 8:29). Because they were exclusively the Lord's, God did for Israel what He did for no other nation (9:4-5).

Finally, it was a calling that *involved responsibility (Amos 3:2b)*. Because He had chosen them, called them, and blessed them, the people of Israel and Judah were responsible to love God and obey Him. If they didn't, God was responsible to chasten them in love and seek to bring them back to Himself.

The doctrine of divine election is not an excuse for sin; rather, it is a motivation for holy living. We should be so humbled by His grace and so amazed at His love (1 John 3:1-2) that our hearts would want to do nothing other than worship and serve Him. Privilege always brings with it responsibility (Eph. 1:3-5; John 15:16; 1 Peter 2:4-5, 9). "For everyone to whom much is given, from him much will be required" (Luke 12:48, NKJV).

As God chosen people, we're to live worthy of our calling (Eph. 4:1) and not follow the practices of the unsaved world (v. 17). This means living in love (5:2), in wisdom (v. 15) and in the Spirit (v. 18). To do anything less is to live beneath our high calling and the privileges we have as the children of God.

2. God called Amos (Amos 3:3-8)

At this point, the people were probably saying, "Who is this rustic farmer that he should preach to us and claim to be God's prophet? What kind of authority does he think he has?" Amos even dared to preach uninvited at the king's chapel at Bethel, where King Jeroboam's chaplain told Amos to go home and preach in Judah (7:10-16).

No doubt when D.L. Moody began to preach, some people said, "What can this uneducated shoe salesman say to us?" And when Billy Sunday began to hold evangelistic campaigns, it's likely that the sophisticated religious crowd asked, "What can this former baseball player teach us?" But God used Moody and Sunday, not in spite of their humble background, but because of it; for He delights to bypass the "wise and prudent" and share His power with "babes" (Luke 10:21).

Amos replied to their ridicule by arguing from effect to cause. If two people want to walk together, they have to appoint a time and place to meet (Amos 3:3). If the lion roars, it's because he's caught his prey (v. 4). If a trap springs, it means the bird has been caught (v. 5); and if the people in a city are terrified, it's because the trumpet has blown, warning them of danger (v. 6). These are obvious facts of life that any thinking person would acknowledge.

Now for the final thrust: If an untrained rustic farmer is preaching God's Word, *it means God has called him*. This isn't a vocation Amos would have chosen for himself; it was chosen for him by the Lord. Amos said, "I was neither a prophet nor a prophet's son, but I was a shepherd, and I also took care of sycamore-fig trees. But the Lord took me from tending the flock and said to me, 'Go, prophesy to My people Israel'" (7:14-15, NIV).

When a prophet proclaims God's Word, it's because the Lord is about to do something important and wants to warn His people (3:7). Review the images Amos used in verses 3-6, and you will see what kind of work God called Amos to do. Because he was walking with God, he knew God's secrets. "The secret of the Lord is with them that fear Him; and He will shew them His covenant" (Ps. 25:14). The lion was roaring. "A lion has roared! Who will not fear? The Lord God has spoken! Who can but prophesy?" (Amos 3:7, NKJV) God was about to spring the trap: Israel would be wiped out by the Assyrians, and Judah would go into exile in Babylon. Amos was blowing the trumpet and preparing the people for the judgment to come.[1]

Amos clearly made his point. It was no accident of vocational choice that he was proclaiming God's message, for God had called him. And it was no accident of international diplomacy that Israel and Judah were facing judgment, for they had sinned against God. For every effect there is a cause. What caused Amos to preach God's Word? The call of God on his life.

Bible history and church history both reveal that God can and does use a variety of people to minister to His people. He used an educated man like Moses, and a humble shepherd like David, a priest like Jeremiah, and common fishermen like Peter, James, and John. Both Charles Finney and C.I. Scofield were trained to be lawyers, while John Bunyan was a mender of pots and pans, and D. Martyn Lloyd-Jones was a physician. Add to this the names of dedicated women God has greatly used—Catherine Booth, "mother" of the Salvation Army; Amy Carmichael, rescuer of abused children; Lina Sandell, Fanny Crosby, and Avis B. Christiansen, composers of beautiful hymns and Gospel songs—and you can see that God calls, equips, and uses all who will surrender to Him and let Him have His way.

Amos is an encouragement to all believers who feel they are inadequate to do the work of the Lord. He was a layman, not a graduate of a prophetic school. He learned spiritual truth as he communed with God while caring for the flocks and orchards. Self-taught? Yes, but he was God-taught; and he was willing to share with others what God had said to him. Robert Murray M'Cheyne wrote, "It is not great talents God blesses so much as great likeness to Jesus." This is not to minimize the importance of either talent or education, but to remind us that neither can be a substitute for heeding God's call and walking in communion with Him. Jesus said, "Apart from Me you can do nothing" (John 15:5, NIV).

3. God calls witnesses (Amos 3:9-10)

In his day, the Prophet Isaiah called heaven and earth to witness against Judah (Isa. 1:2; see Deut. 30:19; 31:28); and Amos summoned the Gentile nations to witness against the Northern Kingdom of Israel whose capital was Samaria. The sin of Israel was so great that it even appalled the pagan nations; for, after all, Israel was sinning against a flood of light (1 Cor. 5:1).

It's tragic and humiliating when the unsaved world catches professed Christians in their sins. It happened to Abraham twice when he lied to heathen kings about his wife Sarah (Gen. 12:10-20; 20:1ff). Samson was shamed before the Philistines (Jud. 16), and David was embarrassed before the king of Gath (1 Sam. 21:10-15). David's adultery with Bathsheba gave "great occasion to the enemies of the Lord to blaspheme" (2 Sam. 12:14). In the late 1980s, the media ministry scandals brought great shame to the church; and whenever a prominent servant of God falls into sin, the news media seem to enjoy telling the story.

Amos called for the Philistines ("Ashdod," Amos 1:8) and the Egyptians to witness what was going on in Samaria (v. 9). The leaders of Israel weren't interested in obeying God's Law and helping the less fortunate. Rather, they were eagerly and unjustly robbing the poor and amassing as much wealth as possible. They built costly houses, filled them with expensive furnishings, and lived in luxury while the poor of the land suffered (3:15; 4:1; 5:11; 6:4-6).

The Law of Moses made it clear that the nation was obligated to care for the widows and orphans, the poor and the strangers in the land (see Ex. 22:25-27; 23:11; Lev. 19:9-15;

25:6, 25-30; Deut. 14:28-29; 15:12-13; 16:11-14). Amos wasn't the only Hebrew prophet to accuse the rich of exploiting the poor and ignoring the needy, for you find similar messages in Isaiah (1:23; 10:1-2), Ezekiel (chap. 34), Micah (2:1-2), and Malachi (3:5).

What a terrible indictment: "They do not know how to do right" (Amos 3:10, NIV). They were so bound by their greed and idolatry that it was impossible for them to do what was right. Like many people today, they were addicted to affluence. They didn't care that others lacked the necessities of life so long as they themselves enjoyed their luxuries. No wonder there was unrest in the land, for the possession of wealth never satisfied the hungers of the heart. "To pretend to satisfy one's desires by possessions," says a Chinese proverb, "is like using a straw to put out a fire."

Even more tragic than their greed was their arrogance. They lived in fortresses so they and their possessions were safe. Like the farmer in one of our Lord's parables (Luke 12:13-21), they thought they were safe and secure, but they discovered that their wealth couldn't stop death from coming. The attitude of the church of Laodicea is prevalent among God's people today: "I am rich, and increased with goods, and have need of nothing" (Rev. 3:17).

4. God calls for judgment (Amos 3:11-15) DEVOURED

Amos announced that the kingdom of Israel would fall to an enemy and the great city of Samaria would be plundered. This happened in 722 B.C. when the Assyrians invaded Israel. The people of Israel had plundered one another, but now a pagan Gentile nation would plunder them. We reap what we sow.

To illustrate what would happen to Israel, Amos borrowed from his experiences as a shepherd. According to Exodus 22:10-13, if a lion takes a sheep and tears it to pieces, the shepherd had to bring remnants of the sheep to prove that it was truly dead (see Gen. 31:39). This would assure the owner of the flock that the shepherd wasn't stealing sheep and lying to his employer. By the time Assyria was through with Israel, only a small remnant of the people would be left. The lion was about to roar! (Amos 1:2; 3:8)

According to 2 Kings 17:5ff, the Assyrians killed some Israelites, took others captive, and then brought into the land captives from other nations, thus producing a people with diverse racial and religious backgrounds. The surviving Jews in the ten tribes of the Northern Kingdom married people who were not Jews, and this produced the people we know as the Samaritans. The "pure" Jews rejected this new "mongrel race" (John 4:9); so the Samaritans set up their own temple and priesthood and established their own religion, which the Lord rejected (vv. 19-24).

Amos made it clear that the invasion of the Assyrians was a work of God, for He was punishing Israel for her sins (Amos 3:14). Why? Because of their selfish luxury and their impudent idolatry. The people resting on their ivory beds in their expensive mansions would be stripped and led off as prisoners of war. The wealthy who had both summer and winter houses would have no houses.

When the Jewish kingdom was divided after the death of Solomon (1 Kings 12), King Jeroboam of Israel didn't want his people going to Jerusalem to worship, lest they go to Judah and never return to Israel. So he established shrines with golden calves at Dan and Bethel, set up his own priesthood, and encouraged the people to worship in Israel. Contrary to the Law of Moses, the king also allowed the people to visit local shrines, where it was more convenient to worship whatever god they chose.

Amos announced that the Lord would destroy the royal chapel at Bethel (Amos 7:13), which indicated that Israel's entire man-made religious system would be demolished.

Nobody would be able to lay hold of the horns of the altar and claim protection (1 Kings 1:50-53), for the horns would be cut off.

For two centuries, God in His long-suffering had tolerated the people of the Northern Kingdom as they participated in their idolatrous rival religious system, but now it would come to an end. Instead of turning to God, however, the remnant in the land would set up another man-made religious system that the Lord would also reject. It would not be until the days of Christ (John 4) and the apostolic church (Acts 8) that the ancient division between Judah and Israel (Samaria) would be healed.

Like Israel of old, nations today measure themselves by their wealth; and the "Gross National Product" becomes the indicator of security and success. The rich get richer and the poor get poorer as people worship the golden calf of money and greedily exploit one another. But it doesn't take long for God to wipe out the idols that people worship and the unnecessary luxuries that control their lives. He hears the cries of the poor and eventually judges the guilty (see Pss. 10:14; 69:33; 82:3).

This isn't the end: Amos has two more messages to deliver.

AMOS 4:1–13

Sins in Good Standing

I accompanied a pastor friend to hear a well-known preach-er, who was visiting the United States. His message was powerful as he named the sins that he felt were destroying our nation.

As we were driving home after the meeting, my friend said, "Well, I must admit that he preached a great message, and it spoke to my heart. But I don't like it when visitors from other countries point out the sins of Americans. There's probably just as much sin back home in their own countries."

I disagreed. After all, God has the right to use whatever servant He chooses to deliver His message wherever He pleases. But I'm sure the people in the kingdom of Israel must have felt the same way as my pastor friend when they heard Amos, a native of Judah, condemning the sins that were destroying Israel. No wonder Amaziah, the priest, told him to go home to Judah! (7:12-13)

In this second message, the Prophet Amos named three particular sins that were grieving the Lord and ruining the kingdom of Israel: luxury (4:1-3), hypocrisy (vv. 4-5), and obstinacy (vv. 6-13). They had the wrong values; their religious "revival" was a sham; and they had refused to listen to the warnings God had given them.

1. Luxury (Amos 4:1-3)

"Most of the luxuries and many of the so-called comforts of life are not only not indispensable, but positive hindrances to the elevation of mankind." So wrote Henry David Thoreau in his classic book *Walden*; and his friend Ralph Waldo Emerson wrote in his own journal, "Our expense is almost all for conformity. It is for cake that we all run in debt." Today, we'd call that "keeping up with the Joneses."[1] Let's seek to answer some questions about luxury.

What is luxury? The word "luxury" comes from a Latin word that means "excessive." It originally referred to plants that grow abundantly (our English word "luxurious"), but then it came to refer to people who have an abundance of money, time, and comfort, which they use for themselves as they live in aimless leisure. Whenever you are offered "deluxe service," that's the same Latin word: service above and beyond what you really need.

It isn't a sin to be rich or to have the comforts of life, if this is God's will for you. Abraham and David were wealthy men. Yet they used what they had for God's glory. In the eyes of people in the Third World, most of the citizens of the Western world, including the poor, are very wealthy. What the Western world considers necessities are luxuries to the citizens of other nations: things like thermostat-controlled heat and air conditioning, refrigerators, automobiles, adequate medical care, telephones, and abundantly available electricity and fuel.

Luxury doesn't mean owning abundant possessions so much as allowing possessions to own us. To live in luxury is to use what we have only for our own enjoyment and to ignore the needs of others. It means being irresponsible in the way we use our wealth, wasting it on futile pleasures instead of using it for the good of others and the glory of God. A sign in an exclusive clothing store read, "If you must ask the price of our garments, you can't afford them." People who live in luxury don't bother to ask the prices. They don't care how much they spend so long as they get what they want.

Who was committing this sin? "Hear this word, you cows of Bashan!"[2] (v. 1, NKJV) Amos addressed the wives of the wealthy leaders of the land, people who had gotten rich by ruthlessly and illegally robbing others. These "society women" lounged around all day, drinking wine and telling their husbands what to do. Any preacher today who called the women in the congregation "cows" would be looking for another church very soon.

Why did Amos, the farmer, use this image? Not because these women were overweight and looked like cows, but because by their sins they were fattening themselves up for the coming slaughter. Both they and their husbands were living in luxury while the poor of the land were suffering because these same men had exploited them and robbed them of money and land.

What will happen to them? What do farmers eventually do with cattle that have been fattened up? They lead them away to be killed and butchered. Amos described what would happen when the Assyrians invaded Israel, how they would capture these women and treat them like cattle. The Assyrian practice was to put hooks in the noses or lower lips of their prisoners, attach ropes, and lead them away like animals, either to captivity or to death. This is what the enemy would do to the wealthy matrons Amos was addressing in his message.[3]

But note that *their posterity* would also be involved in this judgment (v. 2).[4] These wealthy women no doubt wanted "the best" for their children, but by their selfish priorities and their sinful example, they were giving their children the very worst. Their posterity had everything but a knowledge of the Lord; so they too would be led off like animals to the slaughter. The wealthy younger generation in Israel had everything money could buy, but they didn't have the things money can't buy, the things of the Lord that make life worthwhile.

While attending a banquet in Dearborn, Michigan, I found myself seated next to a wealthy gentleman whose name was famous in the business world. In our conversation, I discovered I had some information about a deceased preacher he greatly admired, and I offered to mail it to him. When I asked for an address, I thought he would hand me an expensive embossed calling card. Instead, he gave me a return label ripped off an envelope! I was told that he and his wife lived modestly in spite of their wealth. It's no wonder they were able to give so generously to Christian ministries and philanthropic causes.

Industrial magnate Andrew Carnegie said, "Surplus wealth is a sacred trust which its possessor is bound to administer in his lifetime for the good of the community." Paul wrote, "Command those who are rich in this present age not to be haughty, nor to trust in uncertain riches, but in the living God, who gives us richly all things to enjoy. Let them do good, that they be rich in good works, ready to give, willing to share, storing up for themselves a good foundation for the time to come, that they may lay hold on eternal life" (1 Tim. 6:17-19, NKJV). Paul also quoted Jesus who said, "It is more blessed to give than to receive" (Acts 20:35).

2. Hypocrisy (Amos 4:4-5)

The prophet used "holy irony"[5] when he spoke these words, for he later instructed them to do just the opposite (5:5). It's as though a pastor today said to his congregation, "Sure, go ahead and attend church, but by attending, you're only sinning more. Go and visit the summer Bible conferences, but

Bethel + Gilgal

by doing so, you will be transgressing more. Your heart isn't serious about knowing God or doing His will. Since it's all just playacting. Since it's the popular thing to do, so you do it."

Bethel was a very special place to the Jewish people because of its associations with Abraham (Gen. 12:8; 13:3) Ark and Jacob (28:10-22; 35:1-7). At one time, the ark was kept at Bethel (Jud. 20:18-28), but in Amos' day it was the site of "the king's chapel" where Amaziah, the priest, served (Amos 7:10ff). Gilgal was also important to Israel because that's where Joshua and the people camped when they first entered the Promised Land (Josh. 4:19-20; 5:2-9). Gilgal is also where Saul was made king of Israel (1 Sam. 11:15). Unfortunately, both of these places had become shrines, where the people worshiped pagan gods while claiming to worship the Lord.

On the surface, it looked as if Israel was experiencing a religious revival. Crowds of people were flocking to the "holy places" (Amos 5:5), bringing their sacrifices and tithes (4:4; 5:21-22)[6] and even singing songs of praise to the Lord (v. 23; 6:5; 8:3, 10). They offered sacrifices more frequently than the law required as if to prove how spiritual they were. But their gifts and songs didn't impress the Lord, for He saw what was in their hearts; and the sin in their hearts made their sacrifices unacceptable.

To begin with, their sacrifices were unclean, like offering leaven on the altar, which was forbidden by God (Lev. 2:11; 6:17). God doesn't want the sacrifices of bulls and goats; He wants the obedience of the heart (1 Sam. 15:22-23; see Pss. 50:8-9; 51:16-17; Isa. 1:11-17; Hosea 6:6; Micah 6:6-8; Mark 12:28-34). If the heart isn't right with God, the sacrifice means nothing (Gen. 4:1-7).

Furthermore, they were proud of what they were doing and made sure everybody knew how generous they were to the Lord. They bragged about their freewill offerings, which were purely voluntary; and they boasted to one another of their sacrifices. It wasn't the Lord who got the glory! (See Matt. 6:1-4.) They were like people today who make sure their generosity is recognized from the pulpit and in the church bulletin. If it isn't, they stop giving.

The people of Israel "loved" going to religious meetings, but they didn't love the God they claimed to worship. Making a pilgrimage to Bethel or Gilgal was the popular thing to do in that day, and everybody wanted to keep up with the crowd. There was no confession of sin, no brokenness before the Lord, but only a religious event that made the participants feel good. The whole system was corrupt; the people were sinning when they thought they were serving the Lord.

The application to today's church is obvious. It's very easy for us to join a large happy religious crowd, enthusiastically sing rousing songs, and put money in the offering plate, and yet not be changed in our hearts. The test of a spiritual experience is not "Do I feel good?" or "Did we have a big crowd and a good time?" The real test is "Do I now know God better and am I more like Jesus Christ?"

The people in Amos' day didn't return home determined to help the poor, feed the hungry, and care for the widows and orphans. They went home with the same selfish hearts that they had when they left home, because their "worship" was only an empty ritual (Isa. 1:11-17). Any religious "revival" that doesn't alter the priorities of Christians and help solve the problems in society isn't a "revival" at all.

It's interesting that Amos mentioned music, because that's an important part of the church's worship. However, what the Jews thought was beautiful music, God considered nothing but "noise" (Amos 5:23). People today will pay high prices for tickets to "Christian concerts," yet they won't attend a free Bible study class or Bible conference in their own church. Christian music is big business today, but we wonder how much of it really glorifies the Lord. What we think is music may be nothing but noise to the Lord.

Whether we're looking at the broader religious scene or the services in our local church, it takes spiritual discernment to separate the wheat from the chaff. We need to ask, "Where is prayer in this meeting? Is God getting the glory? Is there a brokenness before Him? Does the fruit remain, or is it gone when the meeting is over and the enthusiasm dies down? Are we overwhelmed by the holiness and the glory of God, or are we just applauding religious celebrities?"

Whether it's evangelism, education, social action, world missions, or feeding the hungry, everything the church accomplishes for the Lord flows out of worship. If the fountainhead of worship is polluted, the church's entire ministry will be defiled. Like the Jews in Amos' day, we're only going to Bethel and sinning! Therefore, it behooves God's people to examine their hearts and make certain that their motives are right and that what they do in public meetings glorifies the Lord.

Amos has dealt with two of the three sins that the Lord told him to condemn—luxury and hypocrisy; and now he deals with the third, obstinacy. God's people were rebellious and hard-hearted, refusing to obey the Lord.

3. Obstinacy (Amos 4:6-13)   *5 times*

Five times in this passage, Amos says to the people, "Yet you have not returned to Me" (4:6, 8, 9, 10, 11, NKJV). The people of Israel experienced God's disciplines, but they wouldn't submit to His will; *and yet they continued practicing their hypocritical religion!* "Not everyone who says to Me, 'Lord, Lord,' shall enter the kingdom of heaven, but he who does the will of My Father in heaven" (Matt. 7:21, NKJV).

God's covenant with the Jews clearly stated that He would bless them if they obeyed His Law and would discipline them if they disobeyed (Deut. 27–29). God set before them life and death, blessing and cursing; and He urged them to choose life (30:19-20). Unfortunately, they spurned His love, rejected His warnings, and chose death.

Consider some of the disciplines that God sent to Israel to bring His people back to Himself.

Famine (Amos 4:6). "Cleanness of teeth" simply means the people had no food to eat. So their teeth didn't get dirty. (The NIV paraphrases it "empty stomachs.") God's covenant promised bumper crops if the people obeyed the Lord, but famine if they disobeyed (Lev. 26:27-31; Deut. 28:1-11). When farmers can't grow crops, food is scarce, food prices go up, and people suffer and die. You would think that this would move people to confess their sins and return to God, but Israel did not return to God.

Drought (Amos 4:7-8). Instead of sending a general drought over the entire kingdom, God withheld the rain in different places from time to time, thus proving that He was in control. This remarkable demonstration of God's sovereign power should have reminded the Jews of what the covenant said about the promised rains (Lev. 26:18-20; Deut. 11:16-17; 28:23-24), but they paid no heed.

Destruction of crops (Amos 4:9). Even when God did allow them to grow fruits and vegetables, they weren't grateful. So He destroyed the crops by sending blight, mildew, and locusts. Once again, God was being true to His covenant warnings (Deut. 28:38-42). So the nation should not have been surprised.

Sicknesses (Amos 4:10a). One of God's promises was that His people would not experience the dreadful diseases they saw in Egypt *if* they were faithful to obey His Law (Ex. 15:26); but if they rebelled against Him, they would suffer all the diseases of Egypt (Lev. 26:23-26; Deut. 28:21-22, 27-29, 35, 59-62). As with the other disciplines, God kept His Word.

Conventional warfare re minister of horses

Defeat in war (Amos 4:10b). "The Lord will cause your enemies who rise against you to be defeated before your face;
they shall come out against you one way and flee before you
seven ways" (Deut. 28:7, NKJV; see Lev. 26:6-8). What a
promise for a small nation surrounded by great empires! But
the promise would be fulfilled only if the people were faithful
to the Lord. If they disobeyed, they would be humiliated and
defeated before their enemies (Lev. 26:32-39; Deut. 28:49-58).
So terrible would be their defeat that the dead bodies in the
camps would not be given decent burial, but would lie there
and rot. God kept His promise: the Assyrians conquered
Israel and the Babylonians took Judah into captivity.

Catastrophe (Amos 4:11). We aren't sure just what this
calamity was. Perhaps it was an earthquake (1:1), or it may
have been the devastating invasion of an army (2 Kings 10:32-
33; 13:7). Whatever it was, it had to be something terrible for
the Lord to compare it to the destruction of Sodom and
Gomorrah (Gen. 19:24-25; see Deut. 29:23; Isa. 1:9; 13:19). The
image of a stick pulled out of the fire suggests that the Lord
intervened and saved them at the last minute (Zech. 3:2).
They had been burned but not consumed. If so, then their
ingratitude and hardness of heart was even more wicked.

Ultimate judgment (Amos 4:12-13). The kingdom of Israel
had experienced famine, drought, blight, plagues, wars, and
devastating catastrophes as God had tried to speak to His
people and bring them to repentance. No matter what discipline He sent, they would not return to Him. What more
could He do? *He could come Himself and deal with them!*
"Prepare to meet thy God, O Israel!" (v. 12) was not a call to
repentance but an announcement that it was too late to
repent. The Lord of Hosts (armies) Himself would come
with the Assyrian hordes and take the people away like cattle
being led to the slaughter (v. 2). "There will be wailing in all
the vineyards, for I will pass through your midst" (5:17, NIV).

41

Amos concluded his message with a doxology of praise to the Lord (4:13; see 5:8-9; 9:5-6). When a servant of God praises the Lord in the face of impending calamity, it shows he's a person of great faith (see Hab. 3:16-19). In this doxology, he reminds us that our God is the Creator who can do anything, including making the earth out of nothing. He can turn dawn into darkness; He can tread upon the mountains, and nobody can hinder Him. He is also the omniscient God who knows what we are thinking. Thus there's nothing we can hide from Him (Ps. 139:1-6). He is the Lord of hosts, the God of the armies of heaven and earth!

This is the God who was coming to judge His people, and they were not prepared!

But are God's people any more prepared today?

AMOS 5:1-17

How to Avoid the Storm

The prophet's third message (5:1–6:14) was a lamentation, a funeral dirge over the death of the nation of Israel. (Israel is mentioned four times in 5:1-4.) "There will be wailing in all the streets," he declares (v. 16, NIV), not just wailing in one or two houses where people have died. Since the people's grief will be so great that there won't be sufficient professional mourners available to express it, they'll call the farmers and workers in the vineyards to help them (vv. 16-17).

However, Amos weaves into his lamentation three pleas to the people, urging them to return to the Lord.

1. "Hear God's Word!" (Amos 5:1-3)

This is the third time Amos has called the people to give attention to God's Word (3:1; 4:1). The way we treat God's Word is the way we treat God, and the way we treat God's messengers is the way we treat the Lord Himself (John 15:18-21). "God . . . has in these last days spoken to us by His Son. . . . See that you do not refuse Him who speaks" (Heb. 1:1-2; 12:25, NKJV).

The listeners must have wondered why Amos was wailing a funeral dirge when nobody in his family or circle of acquain-

tances had died. They were perplexed as to why he was grieving over the death of his nation when the nation seemed to be
prosperous and religious. But the prosperity and "revival"
were only cosmetics to make the sick and dying nation look
healthier. Amos looked at the vital signs, and they were
almost gone. Israel's enthusiastic concerts would become
funerals (5:23; 8:3, 10) and their sacred shrines ruins, for the
Assyrians were destined to destroy the kingdom of Israel.

Amos compared the nation to a virgin daughter in the
bloom of youth, ravaged and slain on the field of battle, her
corpse left to rot.[1] All hope was gone, and nobody could help
her get up. History records the fulfillment of Amos' words.
After the Assyrian invasion, the kingdom of Israel ceased to
exist and has never been restored. Some of the people were
taken into exile, some were slain, and the rest were left to
mingle with the Gentiles that were brought in to resettle the
land. The result was a mixed race—the Samaritans—neither
Jew nor Gentile.

Israel had a strong standing army, but it would be defeated,
and the population decimated, just as the Lord had warned in
His covenant (Lev. 26:7-8; Deut. 28:25; 32:28-30). There can
be no victory when the Lord has abandoned you to your fate,
because you have abandoned Him. Nations today depend on
their wealth, their military establishment, and their political
wisdom when they need to depend on the Lord. "Blessed is
the nation whose God is the Lord" (Ps. 33:12).

Of course, what happened to the Northern Kingdom of
Israel didn't end God's promises to the Jews or His purposes
for them in the world. Groups who claim to be the "ten lost
tribes of Israel" are suspect, because nowhere does Scripture
say the ten tribes were "lost." The New Testament indicates
that God knows where all twelve tribes are (Matt. 19:28;
Luke 22:30; Acts 26:7; James 1:1; Rev. 7:4; 21:12), and the
prophets speak of a time of reunion and glory (Ezek. 37:19-

28; 33:23, 29; Jer. 3:18; 23:5-6; Hosea 1:11).

The first step toward revival and returning to the Lord is to hear what God has to say to us from His Word. "Will You not revive us again, that Your people may rejoice in You? Show us Your mercy, O Lord, and grant us Your salvation. I will hear what God the Lord will speak, for He will speak peace to His people and to His saints; but let them not turn back to folly" (Ps. 85:6-8, NKJV).

2. "Seek the Lord!" (Amos 5:4-6)

This phrase is found more than thirty times in Scripture. It applied to Israel in ancient days, and it applies to God's children today. Even if the whole nation (or church) doesn't respond to the message and return to the Lord, a remnant can return and receive the Lord's help and blessing. God was willing to save the evil city of Sodom if He had found ten righteous people in it (Gen. 18:32); and in Jeremiah's day, the Lord would have been happy to find even one righteous person in Jerusalem! God can work through the many or the few (1 Sam. 14:6), and we should never despise the day of small things (Zech. 4:10).

What does it mean to "seek the Lord"? The Prophet Isaiah answers the question: "Seek the Lord while He may be found, call upon Him while He is near. Let the wicked forsake his way, and the unrighteous man his thoughts; let him return to the Lord, and He will have mercy on him; and to our God, for He will abundantly pardon" (Isa. 55:6-7, NKJV).

To seek the Lord means first of all to change our thinking and abandon the vain thoughts that are directing our wayward lives. Disobedient children of God are thinking wrongly about God, sin, and life. They think God will always be there for them to turn to, but He may abandon them to their sins. They think they can sin and get away with it, but they forget that sinners reap what they sow. To walk "in the counsel of the ungodly" is folly indeed (Ps. 1:1, NKJV), for it leads to a fruitless and joyless life.

When we return to the Lord, we also change direction: We "turn around" and start to move in the right direction. It means forsaking sin and turning to the Lord for mercy and pardon. Until we realize how heinous our sins are in the sight of God, we will never repent and cry out for mercy. To seek the Lord doesn't mean simply to run to God for help when our sins get us into trouble, although God will receive us if we're sincere. It means to loathe and despise the sin in our lives, turn from it, and seek the fellowship of God and His cleansing. "A broken and a contrite heart—these, O God, You will not despise" (Ps. 51:17, NKJV).

Why should we seek the Lord? The prophet gave three reasons, the first of which is *that we might have life (Amos 5:4).* The way of disobedience is the way of darkness and death. "Seek Me and live" is God's invitation and admonition (v. 4, NIV). God disciplines His children in love so that they will repent and return; but if we don't change our ways, He may take our lives. "Moreover, we have all had human fathers who disciplined us and we respected them for it. How much more should we submit to the Father of our spirits and live!" (Heb. 12:9, NIV) The suggestion here is that if we don't submit, we may die; for "there is a sin unto death" (1 John 5:16).

The second reason we should seek God is *because there is no other way to experience spiritual blessing (Amos 5:5).* The people were going to the shrines in droves and coming home further from God than when they left. Emerson said that a change in geography never overcomes a flaw in character, and he was right.

During my years of ministry, I've been privileged to speak at many well-known conference grounds in the United States, Canada, and overseas. I've met people at some of these conferences who actually thought that their physical presence by that lake, in that tent or tabernacle, or on that mountain would change their hearts. They were depending on the "atmosphere" of the conference and their memories of "the good old days" to create a "new spiritual experience" for them, but they usually went home disappointed. Why? Because they didn't seek God.

I'm reminded of a lady at one conference who, when she checked out to go home, asked if she could buy a carton of the soap used in the rooms. When asked why she wanted that particular kind of soap, she explained that it was so rich and lathery, much better than what she used at home. The conference director gave her a carton of the soap, but he didn't have the heart to explain to her that it was the softness of the water, not the formula of the soap, that guaranteed the rich lather.

God doesn't franchise His blessings the way companies franchise their products to local dealers. You can't go to Bethel and Gilgal (see 4:4) or to Beersheba[2] and go home with a blessing in your baggage. Unless we personally meet the Lord, deal with our inner spiritual life, and seek His face, our hearts will never be transformed.

The "holy places" would all be destroyed. The people of Gilgal would go into captivity (5:27), the shrine would be abandoned, and Bethel, the "house of God," would become "Beth Aven," the "house of nothing" (see Hosea 4:15; 5:8; 10:5) and go up in smoke (Amos 5:6). Even if pilgrims traveled into Judah to visit Beersheba, that was no guarantee of blessing. Eventually Judah would fall to the Babylonians.

The third reason for seeking God is because *judgment is coming (v. 6)*. The phrase "lest he break out like fire" reminds us of God's repeated warning in chapters 1 and 2, "I will send a fire" (1:4, 7, 10, 12, 14; 2:2, 5). "For our God is a consuming fire" (Heb. 12:29; see Deut. 4:24). If the Gentiles, who never had the written Law of God, suffered fiery punishment for their sins, how much more would the Jews be punished who possessed God's holy Law! "The Lord shall judge His people" (Heb. 10:30; see Deut. 32:35-36; Ps. 135:14).

Fear of judgment may not be the highest motive for obeying God, but the Lord will accept it. Animals and little children understand rewards and punishments, but we hope that the children will eventually mature and develop higher motives for obedience than receiving some candy or escaping a spanking. God's people, Israel, never achieved that higher level of obedience, the kind of obedience that comes from a heart that loves God (Deut. 4:37; 6:4-6; 7:6-13; 10:12; 11:1; 30:6, 16, 20).

For Israel to repent and return to God was a reasonable thing to do. It would bring them life; it would produce spiritual reality; and it would save them from impending judgment. Those are good reasons for God's people to repent today.

3. "Seek the good!" (Amos 5:7-15)

To "seek the Lord" might appear difficult and distant for some people, an intangible experience they can't get their hands on. Thus Amos brought the challenge down to practical everyday life. He spoke about justice, righteousness, and the importance of telling the truth. He named the sins the people needed to forsake: accepting bribes; charging the poor exorbitant rents; living in luxury while the poor starved; and sustaining a crooked legal system. *True repentance begins with naming sins and dealing with them one by one.*

We must notice that verses 8-9 are a parenthesis in the prophet's message, but a very important parenthesis as he reminded the people of the greatness of their God. Jehovah is the God who created the heavens and the earth, who controls the seasons and the daily motions of the earth, and who is Lord of the heavens, the sea, and the land. The pagan Gentiles worshiped the heavenly bodies, but the Jews were privileged to worship the God who made the heavens and the earth (Jonah 1:9).

But this God of creation is also the God of judgment! "He flashes destruction on the stronghold and brings the fortified city to ruin" (Amos 5:9, NIV). J.B. Phillips graphically translated verse 9, "He it is who flings ruin in the face of the strong, and rains destruction upon the fortress."[3] In the light of the holiness of God and the terms of His holy covenant, the people of Israel should have been on their faces, calling out for mercy. Instead, they were complacently comfortable in their luxury and their sins. Amos named just a few of their sins.

Promoting injustice (Amos 5:7). God established human government because of the sinfulness of the human heart. Without the authority of government in society, everything would fall apart and the strong would enslave the weak and the rich would exploit the poor. Justice is supposed to be "a river . . . a never-failing stream" (v. 24, NIV) that cleanses and refreshes society, but the leaders of Israel had turned that refreshing river into bitter poison (see 6:12).

Righteousness and justice should be the pillars that hold up society, but these selfish rulers had thrown the pillars to the ground. One of the evidences that the pillars of national justice are shaking and ready to fall is the increase in lawsuits. "They make many promises, take false oaths and make agreements; therefore lawsuits spring up like poisonous weeds in a plowed field" (Hosea 10:4, NIV). Israel was afflicted with poisonous weeds and poisonous water (Amos 5:7), and the Lord was displeased.

Instead of running to religious meetings, the people should have stayed home and seen to it that their leaders weren't poisoning the river of justice and knocking down the pillars of righteousness. Christians are the salt of the earth, and salt prevents corruption. They are the light of the world, and if there were more light, there would be less darkness (Matt.

5:13-16). The church must not abandon its marching orders and turn preachers into politicians, but it dare not ignore the problems of society—problems that can be solved by the application of the Gospel and the truth of the Word of God.

Rejecting rebuke (Amos 5:10, 13). The city gate was the place where the elders met and transacted city business (Ruth 4). When the dishonest leaders attempted to foist their lies on the people and manipulate the court, if somebody rebuked them, they turned on that person and tried to silence him or her. It got to the place where the righteous wouldn't say anything because their interference didn't do any good (Amos 5:13). Leaders with integrity will gladly listen to counsel and even to rebuke, but leaders bent on evil will seek to destroy those who stand in their way. "Do not reprove a scoffer, lest he hate you; rebuke a wise man, and he will love you" (Prov. 9:8, NKJV; and see 1 Kings 22:5ff for an illustration of this principle).

For many years, American legal experts have called for an overhaul of the legal system. (Other nations probably have the same or worse problems.) So many cases are pending, and too many trials proceed at a snail's pace, with seemingly interminable appeals and delays, that very little justice results. Isaiah saw a similar situation in his day: "So justice is driven back, and righteousness stands at a distance; truth has stumbled in the streets, honesty cannot enter. . . . The Lord looked and was displeased that there was no justice" (Isa. 59:14-15, NIV). A traffic jam!

Oppressing the poor (Amos 5:11-12). The Prophet Amos was the champion of the poor and the oppressed (2:6-7; 4:1; 8:6) as he called for justice in the land.[4] He pictured the rich trampling the poor into the mud by claiming their crops for payment of the high rents they were charging. The rich were literally taking the food right out of the mouths of their tenants and their children. And if these hungry tenants appealed to the local judges for justice, the wealthy landowners bought off the judges.

So what did the rich do with this ill-gotten wealth? They used it to build mansions for themselves and to plant luxurious vineyards. They anticipated lounging in their big houses and drinking wine, but the Lord had other plans. He announced that they would neither live in their mansions nor drink their wine, because the Assyrians would destroy all their houses and vineyards. Like the selfish rich in the apostolic days, these powerful landowners were fattening their hearts for the day of slaughter (James 5:1-6).

God knew what these wealthy exploiters were doing, just as He knows what sinners are doing today; and though He appeared to be unconcerned, He would judge these evil people in due time. God had warned in His covenant with the Jewish people, "You shall build a house, but you shall not dwell in it; you shall plant a vineyard, but shall not gather its grapes" (Deut. 28:30, NKJV). God always keeps His promises, whether to bless when we've obeyed or to chasten when we've rebelled.

Arrogant self-confidence (Amos 5:14-15). The people were boasting, "The Lord God is with us!" After all, wasn't the nation enjoying great prosperity? Certainly that was a sign of God's blessing. And weren't the people active in religious activities, bringing their sacrifices and offerings to the shrines? And didn't the king have a special priest and a royal sanctuary in Bethel (7:10-17), where he consulted with Amaziah about the affairs of the kingdom?

Yes, these things were true, but they weren't evidence of the blessing of God. They were only a thin veneer of religious self-righteousness over the rotting corpse of the nation. The only proof that God is with us is that we love Him and do His will. Religion without righteousness and justice in the land is hypocrisy. No matter how many people attend religious meetings, if the result is not obedience to God and concern for our neighbor, the meetings are a failure.

How can we claim to love the good if we don't hate the evil? We claim to love the Lord, but God commands, "You who love the Lord, hate evil!" (Ps. 97:10, NKJV) We enjoy studying the Bible, but the psalmist said, "Through Your precepts I get understanding; therefore I hate every false way" (119:104, NKJV). Seeking the good means rejecting the evil *and not being ashamed to take our stand against what's wrong.*

Is there any hope for such a wicked society? Yes, as long as the grace of God is at work. "It may be that the Lord God of hosts will be gracious to the remnant of Joseph" (Amos 5:15, NKJV). Disaster was coming to Israel, but who knows what God would do if only a godly remnant turned to Him and sought His mercy?

"So I sought for a man among them who would make a wall, and stand in the gap before Me on behalf of the land, that I should not destroy it; but I found no one" (Ezek. 22:30, NKJV).

God is still seeking for wall-builders, for intercessors who will plead with God to send revival and renewal to His church. For it's only when God's Spirit is allowed to work among His people that the flood of evil can be stopped and righteousness and justice flourish in the land. The saints want God to judge the wicked, but "the time is come that judgment must begin at the house of God" (1 Peter 4:17).

If only a remnant will repent and turn to God, there is hope that He will send the revival that we desperately need.

"Hear God's Word!" says the prophet. *Are we listening?*

"Seek the Lord!" *Are we praying?*

"Seek the good!" *Do we hate that which is evil?*

There is no other way.

"Woe to the Sinners!"

A mos is still lamenting the impending doom of the nation of Israel. In this section, he pronounces "woe" upon four kinds of people in the kingdom: the ignorant (5:18-27), the indifferent (6:1-2), the indulgent (vv. 3-7), and the impudent (vv. 8-14). The circumstances are different, but we have these same people in the professing church today. Do you recognize them?

1. "Woe to the ignorant!" (Amos 5:18-27)

"The Day of the Lord" is a period of time during which God judges His enemies and establishes His kingdom on earth. It's the answer to our prayer, "Thy kingdom come" and is described in Revelation 6–20 and many passages in the books of the prophets.

The people Amos was addressing saw "the Day of the Lord" as a time of great deliverance for the Jews and terrible punishment for the Gentiles (Joel 2:28-32), but the prophets had a clearer vision of this momentous event. They realized that "the Day of the Lord" was also a time of testing and purifying for Israel (see Isa. 2:10-21; 13:6-13; Jer. 46:10; Joel 3:9-17; Zeph. 2:1-2), when God's people would go through tribulation before entering the kingdom of God.

Amos *looked ahead* and gave three descriptions of "the Day of the Lord." It would first of all be *a day of despair and mourning (Amos 5:18a).* "Woe to you who long for the Day of the Lord!" (NIV) Good theology can lead to hope, but bad theology leads to false hopes. Since these hypocrites were sure that God would spare Israel but condemn their enemies, they longed for the day of the Lord to come. They were like the editors of old editions of the Bible that I've seen: If the chapter was about judgment, the heading read, "God's judgment on the Jews"; but if the chapter was about blessing, the heading read, "God's blessing on the church." Heads we win, tails you lose!

Second, it would be *a day of darkness (vv. 18b, 20).* God had warned that He was about to pass through their midst (v. 17), but not "pass over" as He had in Egypt. This time He was coming to judge His own people; and as there was darkness for three days prior to that first Passover (Ex. 12:12), so "the Day of the Lord" would bring darkness. In addition, what Israel experienced at the hands of the Assyrians was a small sampling of what will happen in the end times when the whole world will see "the Day of the Lord."

Third, it would be *a day of doom (Amos 5:19).* There would be no escaping God's wrath because there were no hiding places! Run from the lion, and you meet the bear; run for safety into your house, and a serpent bites you. We would say, "Out of the frying pan, into the fire!" Remember, God's judgments are very thorough and accurate.

These Israelites were eagerly expecting "the Day of the Lord" without realizing what that day would bring to them. They were like some Christians today who want Jesus to come so they can escape painful situations and not because they "love His appearing" (2 Tim. 4:8). They forget that Christ's return means judgment as well as blessing. "For we must all appear before the Judgment Seat of Christ; that everyone may receive the things done in his body, according to that he hath done, whether it be good or bad. Knowing therefore the terror of the Lord, we persuade men" (2 Cor. 5:10-11).

Next in his message, Amos *looked around (Amos 5:21-24)* and pointed out the sins of the people that made them totally unprepared to experience the Day of the Lord. He began with their *hypocritical worship (vv. 21-22)*, something he had mentioned earlier (4:4-5). They honored special days on the Jewish calendar, called sacred assemblies, offered sacrifices, brought offerings, and sang songs of worship. Their meetings looked so beautiful and holy, yet God not only refused to accept their worship, He said He despised and hated it! (See Isa. 1:10-20.)

The prophet's second indictment was against *their unconcern for others (Amos 5:24)*. This is a key verse in the Book of Amos, for it reveals God's concern that His people be righteous in their character and just in their conduct. We have already noted the emphasis on justice in Amos' messages and how the leaders of the land had turned the pure river of justice into a poisonous stream (5:7; see 6:12). No matter how much "religious activity" we participate in, if we don't love our brother and our neighbor, we can't honestly worship and serve the Lord.

Finally, Amos *looked back (5:25-27)* and reminded them of their relationship to Jehovah after He had delivered them from Egypt. God asked the Jews to give Him faith, obedience, and love; but at Mt. Sinai, after vowing to serve God, the people worshiped a golden calf! (see Ex. 32) Their forefathers sinned further by offering sacrifices to false gods even while Jehovah was leading the nation through the wilderness! (Stephen quotes this in Acts 7:42-43.)[1]

After the Jews settled in the Promised Land, two generations of leaders guided them in the way of the Lord. By the time the third generation came along, however, the people had turned to the idols of the nations around them (Jud. 2:10-15). God had to chasten them by allowing these nations to enslave Israel in their own land. But the message Amos had for the people was that they would have to *leave their land* and go into exile wherever the Assyrians sent them. It meant the end of the Northern Kingdom (2 Kings 17:6ff).

"Where ignorance is bliss," wrote Thomas Gray, "'tis folly to be wise." But the poet was writing about the naive innocence of childhood, not the fatal ignorance of adulthood. He was pleading with adults not to spoil the joys of children by telling them about the burdens of adulthood. However, in the Christian life, ignorance of God's truth keeps us in darkness (Isa. 8:20); so we must understand His "word of prophecy" that shines as a light in this world's darkness (2 Peter 1:19).

2. "Woe to the indifferent!" (Amos 6:1-2)

This "woe" was addressed to both Judah ("Zion") and Israel ("Samaria") because both kingdoms were indifferent toward God's Word and the judgment that was hanging over them. They were calling themselves "the foremost nation" (v. 1, NIV) and enjoying an unwarranted false confidence for several reasons.

The first cause of their complacency was their geography. Situated on Mt. Zion, Jerusalem was considered impregnable (Pss. 78:68-69; 132:13-18); and Samaria also had a seemingly secure position. But when God decided to deal with these cities, nothing could stop the enemy.

As for their prosperity, government, and military strength, Amos had already exposed the folly of depending on them; for the heart of each nation was corrupt to the core. The notable men in Israel's government gave their opinion that the nation was safe and secure, and the people believed them, just as people today believe the political "experts" and the polls. False confidence that's based on expert advice, statistics, and material resources and that ignores the spiritual dimension of life is sure to lead to shameful defeat.

Amos mentioned areas in Syria and Philistia that had already fallen to the Assyrian army and then asked two questions: "Are you better than they? Is your territory bigger than theirs?" If the enemy had already destroyed places bigger and stronger than Samaria and Israel, what hope was there for the Jewish people, especially when the Jews were living like the Gentiles and were disobeying the Lord? God doesn't look at the talent of national leaders, the extent of a nation's army, or the prosperity of its economy. God looks at the heart, and the heart of the two Jewish kingdoms was far from the Lord.

Complacency is an insidious sin, because it's based on lies, motivated by pride, and leads to trusting something other than God (Zeph. 1:12). Like the people in the church of Laodicea, complacent people consider themselves "rich, and increased with goods" and in need of nothing (Rev. 3:17). In reality, however, they have lost everything that's important in the spiritual life. When the Lord sees His people becoming complacent and self-satisfied, He sometimes sends trials to wake them up.

3. "Woe to the indulgent!" (Amos 6:3-7)
"It can't happen here!" was the motto of the complacent leaders. "If a day of judgment is coming, it's surely a long way off." Whenever anybody mentioned the possibility of national disaster, the leaders laughed at the idea and disregarded it. But God had a different viewpoint. He said, "All the sinners of My people shall die by the sword, who say, 'The calamity shall not overtake us, nor confront us'" (9:10, NKJV). Yet by their very indifference, they were bringing the day of judgment that much nearer.

Amos described their indulgent way of life—a way of life that left no place for the disciplines of the spiritual life. They were living for pleasure not for the glory of God. The common people usually slept on mats placed on the ground, but the wealthy enjoyed the luxury of beds of ivory and luxurious couches. They also used ivory to decorate their mansions (3:15). Excavations in Samaria have led to the discovery of the "Samaritan Ivories," fragments of beautiful ivory carvings that once adorned their houses and furniture.

The wealthy also enjoyed elegant feasts, eating lamb and veal, drinking wine in abundance, enjoying beautiful music, and wearing expensive perfumes. The poor people, whom they exploited, couldn't afford to kill tender lambs and calves, but had to settle for occasional mutton and beef, perhaps from a sacrifice. They would serve only cups of wine, not bowls; and their only "cosmetic" was olive oil.[2]

There's certainly nothing wrong with enjoying good food or good music, *provided the things of the Lord are uppermost in your heart*. David designed and made musical instruments, but he used them to praise the Lord. Abraham was able to prepare an elegant feast for his guests (Gen. 18:1-6), and the Lord didn't rebuke him. But the sin in Amos' day was that these luxuries distracted the people from the real problems of the nation, and "they [were] not grieved for the afflictions of Joseph [Samaria]" (Amos 6:6). The NIV translates the Hebrew word *sheber* as "ruin," for it means the total collapse of the nation.

When nations get pleasure-mad, it's a sign that the end is near. Belshazzar and his leaders were enjoying a sumptuous feast when the city of Babylon fell to the Medes and Persians (Dan. 7). The Roman citizens enjoyed free "bread and circuses" as the empire decayed morally and politically and eventually fell to the enemy. One of the marks of the last days is the fact that people become "lovers of pleasures more than lovers of God" (2 Tim. 3:4). No wonder Jesus warned His followers, "But take heed to yourselves, lest your hearts be weighed down with carousing, drunkenness, and cares of this life, and that Day come on you unexpectedly" (Luke 21:34, NKJV).

It's difficult today to find people who are truly burdened about the sins of the nations and the sins of the church. Too many are like the rulers of Samaria or the members of the church of Laodicea, closing their eyes to reality and living on fantasy based on false theology. How many believers can honestly say, "Indignation has taken hold of me because of the wicked, who forsake Your law"? (Ps. 119:53, NKJV) Or, "Rivers of water run down from my eyes, because men do not keep Your law"? (v. 136, NKJV) Too many Christians are laughing when they should be weeping (James 4:8-10) and tolerating sin when they should be opposing it (1 Cor. 5:2).

Dr. Vance Havner told of having dinner in an expensive restaurant with some friends and discovering that the dining room was dimly lighted. At first, he could scarcely read the menu, but then he found he could see fairly well. He said to his friends, "Isn't it strange how easy it is to become accustomed to the dark?" That's one of the problems in the church today: We've gotten accustomed to the darkness, and our lights aren't shining bright enough.

Since these wealthy exploiters of the poor considered themselves to be the first in the land, God said they would be the first to go into captivity (Amos 6:7); for theirs was the greater responsibility. Certainly King Jeroboam and his priest Amaziah, the political and religious leaders of Israel, were among the first to be judged (7:10-17), but their self-indulgent followers eventually had to exchange their lounges for chains and their wine and expensive food for the meager fare of prisoners.

4. "Woe to the impudent!" (Amos 6:8-14)

"I abhor the pride of Jacob, and hate his palaces; therefore I will deliver up the city and all that is in it" (v. 8, NKJV). The Lord not only *said* this, but He also *swore by Himself* to fulfill it, which makes it a most solemn statement. The phrase "pride of Jacob" (KJV says "excellency of Jacob") is used in Psalm 47:4 to mean "the Promised Land."[3] God abhorred the very land of Israel, the land He had given to His people for their inheritance.

Jesus said, "That which is highly esteemed among men is abomination in the sight of God" (Luke 16:15). The people boasted of their fortresses, their mansions, and their elegant way of life, all of which God abhorred and would one day destroy. We're reminded of the destruction of the great Babylonian world system described in Revelation 17–18. People who live without God, whose god is really personal pleasure, will one day hear Him say, "You fool! This night your soul will be required of you; then whose will those things be which you have provided?" (Luke 12:20, NKJV)

These impudent people, who rejected God's warning, would one day face three terrible judgments.

Death (Amos 6:9-10). Amos describes a hypothetical situation to emphasize the terrors that will come when the Assyrians invade Samaria. Ten men, perhaps the remnants of a hundred soldiers (5:3), would be hiding in a house, but pestilence would catch up with them, and they would die. If a relative came to burn the bodies (the safest thing to do in war when disease is rampant), anyone in the house guarding the bodies would deny there were others there who also might die in the plague. But the disposal of the dead bodies wouldn't be a "religious" occasion, for the people would be afraid to even mention the name of the Lord lest He become angry and send more judgment.

Destruction (Amos 6:11-13). Pride always goes before

destruction (Prov. 16:18). The summer houses and winter houses that the wealthy enjoyed and boasted about would one day be nothing but ashes and fragments. The Babylonians would even burn Judah's beautiful temple. This would occur because the Lord commanded it, and His commands are always obeyed.

The prophet argues from the order of nature (Amos 6:12). Horses are too wise to gallop on slick rocks, where they might slip and fall. Farmers are too wise to try to plow the rocks or the sea,[4] because the plow won't accomplish anything on rocks or water. (Remember, Amos was a farmer.) Plain common sense convinces us of the truth of these statements. Then why would God's people poison their own judicial system? What they did just didn't make sense!

Their pride again came to the fore when they boasted of their military victories at Lo-Debar and Karnaim (see NKJV or NIV). We aren't certain when Israel took these cities, and it's not important. What is important is that they were proud of their achievements and confident that nobody could defeat them. Lo-Debar means "nothing," and that's what God thought of their victory! They boasted that the victory came because of their own strength, and their false confidence would lead to their destruction.

Disgrace and defeat (Amos 6:14). If a nation rehearses the victories of the past and gives the glory to God, that's one thing, but if they claim the victory for themselves, they are asking only for future defeat. Humble dependence on God is the only guarantee of His help and blessing.

Assyria's invasion of Israel wouldn't take place because of the accidents or incidents of international politics. *God* would bring the army into the land and give Assyria the responsibility of chastening His people. "'Behold, I will bring a nation against you from afar, O house of Israel,' says the Lord" (Jer. 5:15, NKJV).

Hamath is in the north of Israel, and the river of the Arabah is in the south. Thus this means that Assyria would devastate the entire land. At the time Amos spoke those words, Assyria was a rather weak nation; and King Jeroboam was able to keep Assyria, Egypt, and Syria at bay. But that would change, and Assyria would become a threatening world empire. After all, it is God who controls the nations and assigns them their lands (Acts 17:26).

The Prophet Amos has finished preaching his three messages to the proud and complacent kingdom of Israel. He has looked within their hearts and exposed the corruption there. Now the Lord will give His servant six visions—five visions of judgment and one of the glorious kingdom that will be established after the Day of the Lord. With the record of these visions, Amos will close his book.

S I X

Stop—Look—Listen!

The prophecy of Amos concludes with the record of five special visions of judgment that God gave to His servant: the locusts (7:1-3), the fire (vv. 4-6), the plumb line (vv. 7-9), the basket of fruit (8:1-14), and the ruined temple (9:1-10). However, the prophet closes his message on a positive note as he describes the future glorious kingdom that God has promised to His people (vv. 11-15).

But these visions center around three experiences of the prophet in which Amos *struggles* with God and men (chap. 7), *declares* that judgment is coming (chap. 8) and *affirms* that God is working out His perfect plan (chap. 9).

1. The prophet struggles (Amos 7:1-17)

The life of a prophet wasn't easy. On the one hand, he had to stay close to the Lord in order to hear His words and be able to share them with the people. But on the other hand, he also had to be with the people to whom he was ministering, and they didn't always want to accept his ministry. It's no wonder that some of the prophets wanted to resign, including Moses and Jeremiah. Amos had two struggles: one with the Lord and one with the authorities, especially the king and his priest. When you read the Book of Acts, you see that the apostles also faced struggles with the religious establishment and with the government.

Struggling with the Lord (Amos 7:1-9). Amos was a true patriot who loved God and loved his nation, and it grieved him that he had to tell Israel and Judah that judgment was coming. No doubt there were times when he wished he was back at Tekoa caring for the sycamore trees and the sheep. But the Sovereign Lord ("Lord God," used eleven times in these three chapters) was in control of history, and Amos knew that God's will was best. The prophet saw three visions of judgment and responded to them.

First, Amos saw the *vision of the locusts (vv.1-3)* as they were poised to attack the second crop late in the summer, after the king had taken his share (1 Kings 4:7). This was the farmers' last chance for a harvest, and the harvest would be destroyed. The summer heat was on its way, and there would be no more chance for a crop. Being a man of the soil himself, Amos would sympathize with these farmers.

The strange thing is that it was *God* who prepared these insects and told them what to do! It was as though He turned against His own people and deliberately planned to strip their fields of food. But since the heart of Amos agonized for his people, he prayed that the Lord would call off the judgment; and He did. Amos joined that select group of intercessors, which included Abraham (Gen. 18), Moses (Ex. 32; Num. 14), Samuel (1 Sam. 12), Elijah (1 Kings 18), and Paul (Rom. 9:1-3; 10:1-2).

Amos argued that the nation was so small that they could never survive the plague of locusts. Amos didn't plead any of the covenant promises of God because he knew the people had violated God's covenant and were deserving of a plague (Deut. 28:38-42). But God heard the prophet's plea and relented (Joel 2:12-14).[1]

The second vision was that of *the devouring fire (Amos 7:4-6)* in which the fire dried up the water and burned the land. The image is that of a great drought, and Amos had mentioned a drought earlier (4:7-8). God's judgment so moved the prophet that he cried out to the Lord and begged Him to cease, and once more God relented.

The third vision was that of *the plumb line (Amos 7:7-9)*, an instrument used to test whether a wall was straight and true. A man stood on top of the wall and dropped a line with a weight on it. By matching the line to the wall, the workers could tell if the wall was upright.

God's Law is His plumb line, and He measures His people to see how true they are to the pattern in His Word, and if they are upright in character and conduct. "Also I will make justice the measuring line, and righteousness the plummet" (Isa. 28:17, NKJV). Alas, in Amos' time, He found that Israel was "out of plumb" and therefore had to be destroyed. This would include Israel's high places and sanctuaries, where they worshiped contrary to God's law, for the only place the Jews were to bring their sacrifices was to the temple in Jerusalem (Lev. 17:1-7).

"I will spare them no longer" was certainly an ominous statement. The nation had gone too far, and now there was no hope. For this reason, Amos didn't intercede for the land as he had done twice before. Like Jeremiah, he did not pray for the people (Jer. 7:16; 11:14; 14:11).

Struggling with the authorities (Amos 7:10-17). Israel's main sanctuary was at Bethel; it was the king's chapel. God had told Amos that the sanctuary would be destroyed and that King Jeroboam II would be slain. This wasn't an easy message to proclaim, for Amos was attacking both the government and the religion of the nation. Yet he faithfully went to Bethel and preached the Word. Four different messages were involved in this event.

The first message was *Amaziah's report to the king (vv. 10-11)*. Since the king had appointed Amaziah, he had an obligation to tell the king what the farmer preacher was saying to the people. The king didn't bother to go hear Amos himself, although it would have done him good to listen and obey. Jeroboam was very comfortable and complacent and wasn't about to have some visiting farmer tell him what to do.

The second message was *Amaziah's message to Amos (vv. 12-13)*. Of course, Jeroboam II didn't want to hear that his chapel and shrines would be destroyed, that he would die, and that the Assyrians would exile his people. Such a pessimistic message had to be silenced. Thus the king told his priest to tell Amos to go home where he belonged.

Amaziah's words to Amos reveal the wicked attitudes in the priest's heart. He called Amos a "seer," which in this case means "a visionary." He claimed that there was no validity to Amos' message; he only dreamed it up. Then the priest suggested that Amos was also a coward, who would run away if the king began to deal with him. He hinted that Amos was a hireling prophet, who was part of a conspiracy and was interested only in earning bread. Finally, Amaziah told Amos to get out and stay out because the king's chapel was for the elite, and he was nothing but a common farmer who thought he was a prophet. It was a bitter speech that might have cut the prophet deeply.

It's not unusual to find conflicts between priests and prophets in the Old Testament. (Of course, Amaziah was a false priest and not a true servant of God.) Actually, both prophets and priests were needed in the land, because the priests "conserved" the ancient religious traditions, while the prophets applied the Word to the present situation and called people back to God. There were false prophets, who taught lies and sometimes worked with the priests to maintain the status quo, and the true prophets, who had to oppose both priests and false prophets. In Israel, there were false priests who had no valid connection with the levitical priesthood (see Isa. 1:12-15; Jer. 7:1-11; Ezek. 34:1ff; Hosea 4:4-9).

Now we listen to the *prophet's message to the priest (Amos 7:14-16)*. First, Amos revealed the kind of man he was by not being intimidated or running away. Like Nehemiah, he could say, "Should such a man as I flee?" (Neh. 6:11) To run away would be to agree with all the accusations and insinuations the false priest had made. Then Amos told Amaziah what he was: a prophet called by God. In his native Judah, he did not work as a prophet but as a herdsman and a tender of sycamore trees. He didn't make himself a prophet, nor was he a "son of the prophets," that is, a student in one of the prophetic schools (1 Kings 2:35; 2 Kings 2:3, 5, 7, 15). God had called him, and he obeyed the call.

Amos then proclaimed the Word of the Lord to Amaziah and informed him of the judgment that God would send on him and his family. Amaziah would lose all his property, go into exile, and die far from his native land. The Assyrian soldiers would slay his sons. His wife would be left destitute and would become a prostitute. The nation of Israel would go into exile and be no more. It would be quite a change from serving as the king's chief religious leader at Bethel!

Amaziah had position, wealth, authority, and reputation, but Amos had the Word of the Lord. Amaziah served the king of Israel and depended on him for support, but Amos served the King of Kings and had no fear of what men could do to him. Many times in the history of the church, God has called humble instruments like Amos to declare His Word; and we had better be prepared to listen and obey. It's not the approval of the "religious establishment" that counts, but the calling and blessing of the Lord.

2. The prophet declares (Amos 8:1-14)

After his painful encounter with Amaziah, Amos received further messages from the Lord; for it's just like the Master to encourage His servants after they've been through tough times (see Acts 18:9-11; 27:21-26; 2 Tim. 4:16).

The end is coming (Amos 8:1-3). God often used common objects to teach important spiritual truths, objects like pottery (Jer. 18–19), seed (Luke 8:11), yeast (Matt. 16:6, 11), and in this text, a basket of summer (ripe) fruit. Just as this fruit was ripe for eating, the nation of Israel was ripe for judgment. The Hebrew word translated "summer" or "ripe" in verse 1 (*qayis*) is similar to the word translated "end" in verse 2 (*qes*). It was the end of the harvest for the farmers, and it would be the end for Israel when the harvest of judgment came (see Jer. 1:11-12 for a similar lesson). "The harvest is past, the summer is ended, and we are not saved" (Amos 8:20).

There comes a time when God's long-suffering runs out (Isa. 55:6-7) and judgment is decreed. The songs at the temple[2] would become funeral dirges with weeping and wailing and corpses would be thrown everywhere and not given proper burial. It would be a bitter harvest for Israel as the nation reaped what it sowed. People would be so overwhelmed that they would be unable to discuss the tragedy. Silence would reign in the land.

Why the end is coming (Amos 8:4-6). The reason was simple: Israel had broken God's Law and failed to live by His covenant. The first table of the Law has to do with our relationship to God and the second table with our relationship to others, and Israel had rebelled against both. They did not love God, and they did not love their neighbors (Matt. 22:36-40).

They trampled on the poor and needy and robbed them of the little they possessed (Amos 8:4), an indictment that Amos had often brought against the people (2:6-7; 4:1; 5:11-12). When they did business, the merchants used inaccurate measurements so they could rob their customers. The Law demanded that they use accurate weights and measures (Lev. 19:35-36; Deut. 25:13-16), but they cared only for making as much money as possible.

Added to their deception was their desecration of the Sabbath and the religious holy days. The worship of God interrupted their business, and they didn't like it! You might expect Gentile merchants to ignore the holy days (Neh. 13:15-22), but certainly not the Jewish merchants. The poor were unable to pay for the necessities of life and had to go into servitude to care for their families, and the merchants would have them arrested for the least little offense, even their inability to pay for a pair of shoes.

These evil vendors would not only alter their weights and measures and inflate their prices, but they would also cheapen their products by mixing the sweepings of the threshing floor with the grain. You didn't get pure grain; you got the chaff as well. "For the love of money is a root of all kinds of evil" (1 Tim. 6:10, NIV).

How the end is coming (Amos 8:7-14). The prophet used four pictures to describe the terror of the coming judgment. The first was that of *an earthquake (v. 8)* with the land heaving like the rising waters of the Nile River. (The Nile rose about twenty-five feet during its annual flooding stage.) Even the land would shudder because of the people's sins. Earlier Amos referred to an earthquake (1:1), but we aren't sure whether it was the fulfillment of this prophecy.

God would also visit them with *darkness (Amos 8:9),* perhaps an eclipse. (There was one in 763 B.C.) The Day of the Lord will be a day of darkness (Isa. 13:9-10; Joel 2:30-31).

The third picture is that of *a funeral (Amos 8:10),* with all their joyful feasts turned into mourning and wailing. Instead of being dressed elegantly and going to banquets or concerts, the people would wear sackcloth and join in mourning.

Parents would mourn greatly if an only son died because that would mean the end of the family name and line. But God's judgment would mean the end of a nation.

Finally, the judgment would be like *a famine (vv. 11-14)*, not only of literal food but also of spiritual nourishment. "Man shall not live by bread alone, but by every word that proceeds from the mouth of God" (Matt. 4:4, NKJV; see Deut. 8:3). In times of crisis, people turn to the Lord for some word of guidance or encouragement; but for Israel, no word would come. "We are given no miraculous signs; no prophets are left, and none of us knows how long this will be" (Ps. 74:9, NIV).

What a tragedy to have plenty of "religion" but no Word from the Lord! That means no light in the darkness, no nourishment for the soul, no direction for making decisions, no protection from the lies of the enemy. The people would stagger like drunks from place to place, always hoping to find food and drink for their bodies and spiritual sustenance for their souls.

3. The prophet affirms (Amos 9:1-15)

In this final chapter of the book, the Prophet Amos shares four affirmations from the heart of the Lord—three of which deal with judgment and the fourth with mercy.

"I will strike!" (Amos 9:1) In a vision, Amos saw the Lord standing by an altar and announcing that the worshipers would be slain because the building would be destroyed and fall upon them. This was probably not the temple in Jerusalem because Amos was sent to the Northern Kingdom of Israel; and when the Babylonians destroyed the temple in Jerusalem, it was by fire (Jer. 52:12-13). This may have been the king's royal chapel at Bethel, although we don't know what kind of building that was. God's warning in Amos 3:13-15 seems to parallel this vision, describing what the Assyrian army would

do when it entered the land.

The altar was the place of sacrifice and atonement, but God refused to accept their sacrifices and forgive their sins (5:21-23). Their man-made religion, carried on by unauthorized priests, was an abomination to the Lord; and He would now destroy it.

"I will search!" (Amos 9:2-4) Any idolatrous worshiper who tried to escape would be tracked down and slain. Though they dug down into sheol, the realm of the dead, God would search them out; and if they could reach heaven, there would be no protection there. They couldn't hide from God on the highest mountain or in the depths of the sea (see Ps. 139:7-12). Even if they were taken captive to a foreign land, He would find them and judge them. His eye would be upon them for judgment, not for blessing (33:18; 34:15; Rev. 6:12-17).

"I will destroy!" (Amos 9:5-10) Nine times in his book, Amos calls God "the Lord of hosts," that is, "the Lord of the armies of heaven and earth." A.W. Tozer correctly says, "The essence of idolatry is the entertainment of thoughts about God that are unworthy of Him."[3] The people of Israel created their gods in their own image and held such a low view of Jehovah that they thought He would approve of their sinful ways.

Amos reminded them of the greatness of the God they thought they were worshiping. He is the God of creation, who can melt the earth with a touch and make the land rise and fall like the swelling of the Nile River. He controls the heavens, the earth, and the seas, and no one can stay His hand.

Jehovah is the God of history, who showed His great power by delivering the Jews from the bondage of Egypt (v. 7). He claimed them for His own people. Yet they turned against Him and went their own way. Therefore, He will have to treat the Jews (His special people) as He treats the Gentiles! The exodus from Egypt will be looked upon like any migration of a people from one place to another, for the people of Israel gave up their national distinctives when they abandoned the worship of the true God.

But He is always the God of mercy (vv. 8-10), who will keep His covenant with Abraham and his descendants and not destroy the nation. The nation would be sifted, and the sinners punished, but not one of His true worshipers would be lost. It's always the believing remnant that God watches over so that they might fulfill His will on the earth. The self-confident sinners, who don't expect to be punished, are the ones who will be slain by the sword (v. 10).

"I will restore!" (Amos 9:11-15) In contrast to God's destroying the Israelite house of false worship, God will raise up the "hut" of David, thereby assuring a bright future for the people of Israel and Judah. Like a rickety shack, David's dynasty was about to collapse. From the Babylonian Captivity to this present hour, there has been no Davidic king ruling over the Jews; and though a Jewish nation has been restored, they have no king, priest, temple, or sacrifice.

But one day, the Lord will restore, repair, and rebuild the dynasty of David and establish the kingdom He promised. When Jesus Christ comes again, the breach between Israel and Judah will be healed, and there will be one nation submitted to one King. God will bless the land and the people, and His people shall live in peace and security.[4] It will be a time of peace and prosperity to the glory of the Lord.

Amos ends his prophecy with the wonderful promise that Israel shall be planted, protected, and never again pulled up from her land "says the Lord your God." *Your God!* What a great encouragement for the Jews to know that, in spite of their unbelief, their God will be faithful to keep His covenant promises.

Obadiah in His Time

We know very little about the Prophet Obadiah except that he wrote the prophecy bearing his name (the shortest book in the Old Testament) and that his name means "one who worships God." At least twelve other men in Scripture had this name, four of whom were connected in some way with the ministry at the temple (1 Chron. 9:16; 2 Chron. 34:12; Neh. 10:5, 12:25).

Students aren't even agreed as to when the events occurred that are described in Obadiah 10-14. The traditional view is that Obadiah was referring to the Babylonian invasion of Judah and the destruction of Jerusalem in 586 B.C. The psalmist states that the Edomites encouraged the Babylonians as the army razed the city (Ps. 137:7), but there is no evidence that the Edomites actually entered Jerusalem at that time or tried to stop the Jews from escaping.

Some Old Testament scholars think that Obadiah's reference is to an earlier invasion of Jerusalem by the Philistines and Arabians, at which time Edom assisted the invaders and broke free from Judah's control (2 Chron. 21:8-10, 16-17). This would have been during the reign of weak King Jehoram (853–841), who married King Ahab's daughter and led Judah into sin. God permitted the invasion of the land and the plundering of Jerusalem as a punishment for the king's disobedience.

Obadiah's themes are: (1) the evil of long-standing family feuds, (2) the certainty that people eventually suffer for the way they treat others, and (3) the assurance that Israel's enemies will be defeated and the kingdom established in the land.

A Suggested Outline of the Book of Obadiah

Key theme: Nations and individuals reap what they sow
Key verse: Obadiah 15

I. God's message to Edom's neighbors—1
A call to arms against their old ally.

II. God's message to Edom—2-16
1. Divine judgment declared—2-9
(1) Edom's pride brought down—2-4
(2) Edom's wealth plundered—5-6
(3) Edom's alliances broken—7
(4) Edom's wisdom destroyed—8
(5) Edom's army defeated—9
2. Divine judgment defended—10-16
(1) Violence against the Jews—10-11
(2) Rejoicing at the Jews' plight—12
(3) Assisting the enemy—13-14
(4) Ignoring God's wrath—15-16

III. God's message to the Jewish people—17-21
1. God will deliver them—17-18
2. God will defeat their enemies—19-20
3. God will establish their kingdom—21

S E V E N

A *Tale of Two Brothers*

Of all human conflicts, the most painful and difficult to resolve are those between blood relatives. But if family feuds are tragic, national feuds are even worse. Almost every nation has experienced a civil war, with brother killing brother in order to perpetuate a long-standing disagreement that nobody fully understands or wants to settle. History records that the roots of these disputes are bitter, long, and deep, and that every attempt to pull them up and destroy them usually meets with failure.

Esau and Jacob were twin brothers who had been competitors from before birth (Gen. 25:19-26). Unfortunately, their parents disagreed over the boys, with Isaac partial to Esau and Rebekah favoring Jacob. God had chosen Jacob, the younger son, to receive the blessing attached to the Abrahamic Covenant (Rom. 9:10-12), but Jacob and Rebekah decided to get this blessing by scheming instead of by trusting God (Gen. 27).

When Esau learned that his clever brother had stolen the blessing, he resolved to kill him after their father was dead, and this led to Jacob's leaving home to find a wife among his mother's relatives (vv. 41-46). Years later, the two brothers

75

experienced a brief time of reconciliation (Gen. 32), and they both faithfully attended to the burial of Isaac (35:27-29), but the animosity was never removed. Esau established the nation of Edom (25:30; 35:1, 8; 36:1ff), and his descendants carried on the family feud that Esau had begun years before.[1]

The Law of Moses commanded the Jews to treat the Edomites like brothers: "You shall not abhor an Edomite, for he is your brother" (Deut. 23:7, NKJV). In spite of this, the Edomites "harbored an ancient hostility" against Israel (Ezek. 35:5, NIV) and used every opportunity to display it.

In this brief book, Obadiah the prophet delivered three messages from the Lord.

1. God's message to Edom's neighbors (Obad. 1)
Like Isaiah (1:1), Micah (1:1), Nahum (1:1), and Habakkuk (1:1), the Prophet Obadiah received his message from the Lord by means of a vision. "Surely the Lord God does nothing unless He reveals His secret counsel to His servants the prophets" (Amos 3:7, NASB). Obadiah wrote the vision so it could be shared with others and eventually become a part of the Holy Scriptures.

The Lord enabled Obadiah to know what was going on among the nations that were allied with Edom against Judah. Thanks to today's international media coverage and the instant transmission of information, very little can happen in political and diplomatic arenas without the world knowing about it. But in Obadiah's day, the travels of national leaders and their political discussions were secret. There were no newspapers or press conferences.

God told His servant that an ambassador from a nation allied with Edom was visiting the other nations to convince their leaders to join forces and attack Edom. Actually, it was the Lord who had ordained this change in policy, and what appeared to be just another diplomatic visit was actually the working out of the Lord's judgments against Edom. This was the beginning of the fulfillment of the prophecy in Obadiah 7, "All your allies will force you to the border" (NIV).

John Wesley is said to have remarked that he read the newspaper "to see how God was governing His world," and this is certainly a biblical approach. God rules over kingdoms and nations (2 Chron. 20:6; Dan. 5:21); and as A.T. Pierson used to say, "History is His story." This doesn't mean that God is to blame for the foolish or wicked decisions and deeds of government officials, but it does mean that He is on the throne and working out His perfect will.

The eminent British historian Herbert Butterfield said, "Perhaps history is a thing that would stop happening if God held His breath, or could be imagined as turning away to think of something else." The God who knows the number and the names of the stars (Ps. 147:4) and who sees when the tiniest bird falls dead to the ground (Matt. 10:29) is mindful of the plans and pursuits of the nations and is working out His divine purposes in human history.

Knowing that the Lord reigns over all things ought to encourage the people of God as we watch world events and grieve over the decay of people and nations. The sovereignty of God isn't an excuse for believers to be indifferent to evil in the world, nor is it an encouragement to slumber carelessly and do nothing. God's ways are hidden and mysterious, and we sometimes wonder why He permits certain things to happen, but we must still pray "Thy will be done" (Matt. 6:10) and then be available to obey whatever He tells us to do.

2. God's message to Edom (Obad. 2-16)

There are two parts to this message. First, the prophet declared that God would judge Edom and take away everything the nation boasted about and depended on for security (vv. 2-9). Second, Obadiah explained why God was judging

Edom and named four ways in which the Edomites had sinned against the Jews and the Lord (vv. 10-16).

Divine judgment declared (Obad. 2-9).[2] What kind of judgment did God promise to send to the nation of Edom? To begin with, He said He would *bring down their pride (vv. 2-4)*. Edom was a proud nation that considered itself impregnable and invulnerable because it was situated "in the clefts of the rock" (v. 3), a region of rugged mountains with high cliffs and narrow valleys that would dissuade any invader from attacking. Like the eagles, the Edomites lived on the rocks and looked down from the heights with disdain upon the nations around them. The Edomites thought they were a great people, but God said He would make them small, which means "paltry." "Pride goes before destruction, a haughty spirit before a fall" (Prov. 16:18, NIV).

The prophet also said that *their wealth would be plundered (Obad. 5-6)*. Located on several major trade routes, Edom could amass the riches of other nations; and out of their mountains, they could dig copper and other minerals. Because of their isolation, they didn't have to worry about making treaties with the larger nations or helping to finance expensive wars. But their wealth would be no more. Unlike ordinary thieves, their plunderers would take everything they could find; and unlike grape harvesters, they would leave nothing behind for others. This would be the end of Edom and its boasted wealth.

Third, the Lord would work so that *their alliances would be broken (v. 7)*. Though protected by their lofty heights, the Edomites were smart enough to know that they needed friends to help them stand against the great empires that frequently threatened the smaller eastern nations. Edom would also want allies to assist them in their constant feud with Israel (see Ps. 83:5-8). But God would turn these friends into enemies, and those who had eaten bread with them and made covenants of peace would break those covenants. While pretending to be friends, their allies would turn into traitors, set a trap, and catch Edom by surprise.

Nations today that boast of their political alliances and their formidable military establishments should take heed to what happened to Edom long ago, for that proud nation is no more. About 300 B.C., the Nabataean Arabs drove out the Edomites and occupied their key city Petra, the "rose red city" carved out of solid rock. The Romans took Petra in A.D. 105, but the decline in the caravan routes eventually led to the nation's demise.

God also warned that *Edom's wisdom would be destroyed (Obad. 8)*. The people of the east were known for their wisdom (1 Kings 4:30), and this included the Edomites. Located as they were on the great trade routes, the leaders of Edom could get news and views from many nations. Job's friend Eliphaz was from Teman in Edom (Job 2:11; see Jer. 49:7). Without wisdom, the leaders of Edom couldn't make the right decisions, and the result would be confusion.

Finally, Obadiah announced that *Edom's army would be defeated (Obad. 9)*. Without wisdom, the military leaders wouldn't know how to command their troops, and their mighty men would be defeated. This may have happened when the Babylonians took Jerusalem, or this promise may have been fulfilled when the Arabs invaded Edom and took over their cities, driving the Edomites to the west. The Greeks and Romans called these Edomites "Idumeans" (Mark 3:8), and from them came Herod the Great.

Having announced what God was going to do to Edom, Obadiah then proceeded to *defend God's judgment of the nation (Obad. 10-16)*. The Edomites were guilty of at least four abominable sins, the first of which was *using violence against their brothers, the Jews (vv. 10-11)*. When their founder Esau discovered he was deprived of his father's blessing, he determined to kill his brother Jacob (Gen. 27:41), and this malicious attitude was passed along to his descendants. If you had asked them, "Are you your brother's keeper?" they would have replied, "No! We're our brother's killer!"

Instead of assisting their brothers in their plight, the Edomites stood "on the other side" (see Luke 10:30-32) and watched the enemy soldiers cast lots for the spoils, including the captive Jews, who would become slaves. The Edomites acted like the enemy instead of behaving like blood brothers of the Jews.

A word from Solomon is appropriate here: "Deliver those who are drawn toward death, and hold back those stumbling to the slaughter. If you say, 'Surely we did not know this,' does not He who weighs the hearts consider it? He who keeps your soul, does He not know it? And will He not render to each man according to his deeds?" (Prov. 24:11-12, NKJV) Also, a word from the Prophet Amos: "For three sins of Edom, even for four, I will not turn back My wrath. Because he pursued his brother with a sword, stifling all compassion, because his anger raged continually and his fury flamed unchecked" (Amos 1:11, NIV).

Not only did the Edomites ignore the plight of the Jews, but also *they rejoiced at what the enemy was doing (Obad. 12; see Ezek. 35:15; 36:5)*. For the Jews, this was a day of destruction and distress; but for the Edomites, it was a day of delight and rejoicing. In their pride, Edom looked down on the Jews and gloated over their misfortune. Again, Solomon has counsel for us: "Do not gloat when your enemy falls; when he stumbles, do not let your heart rejoice, or the Lord will see and disapprove and turn His wrath away from him" (Prov. 24:17-18, NIV). God didn't spare the Jews but He did send judgment on Edom in due time.

Edom's third great sin was *assisting the enemy in attacking the Jews (Obad. 13-14)*. It was bad enough for people to do nothing to help their brothers, and to stand and rejoice at their brothers' calamities, but when they gave aid to the enemy, that was carrying their ancient "family feud" too far. The Edomites entered the city and shared in dividing up the spoils, thus robbing their brothers of their wealth. (Later, Edom's wealth would be taken.) The Edomites also stood at the forks in the roads, ready to capture the fugitives who were trying to escape; and they turned them over to the enemy to be imprisoned or slain.

What the Prophet Jehu asked King Jehoshaphat is applicable here: "Should you help the wicked and love those who hate the Lord and so bring wrath on yourself from the Lord?" (2 Chron. 19:2, NASB) As God's people, we must love our enemies and pray for them (Matt. 5:44-48), but we certainly shouldn't assist sinners in opposing and persecuting believers. To do so is to turn traitor in the army of the Lord.

Edom's fourth sin was that of *ignoring the impending wrath of God (Obad. 15-16).* "For the day of the Lord draws near on all the nations" (v. 15, NASB), and that included Edom, but Edom was proud and didn't care about what the Lord might do to them. "The Day of the Lord" is a phrase that describes the time when God will pour His wrath out upon a wicked world, judge the nations, and then establish His kingdom, thus fulfilling the promises made to Israel.[3] However, the phrase was also used to describe God-ordained calamities sent to punish people at any time, and these judgments were foretastes of the future worldwide "Day of the Lord."

"Therefore, whatever you want men to do to you, do also to them, for this is the Law and the Prophets" (Matt. 7:12, NKJV). We call this statement "The Golden Rule," and it points out a positive approach to personal relationships. But Obadiah 15 gives the negative side: "As you have done, it will be done to you. Your dealings will return on your own head" (NASB). Or, as Paul expressed it, "Do not be deceived, God is not mocked; for whatever a man sows, that he will also reap" (Gal. 6:7, NKJV).

Edom had drunk in joyful celebration at Jerusalem's fall, but all the nations will one day drink of the cup of wrath that God will hand them—a cup they cannot refuse (see Isa. 51:17, 21-23; Jer. 25:15-33). No matter how discouraging the day may be for God's people, there is a just God in heaven who pays sinners back in kind: What they did to others is ultimately done to them. Since Pharaoh ordered all the Jewish boy babies drowned, God drowned the Egyptian army (Ex. 1; 14:26-31). The men who lied about Daniel in order to have Daniel thrown to the lions were themselves thrown to the lions (Dan. 6). The unbelievers on earth who shed the blood of God's servants will one day drink water turned into blood (Rev. 16:5-6). "The righteous is delivered from trouble, and it comes to the wicked instead" (Prov. 11:8, NKJV). Indeed, God's judgments are true and righteous (Rev. 16:7).

3. God's message to the Jewish people (Obad. 17-21)
Now that the prophecy about Edom has been delivered, Obadiah turns to His own people and announces three divine promises.

God will deliver you (Obad. 17-18). God did deliver His people from Babylonian Captivity, and He will again deliver them in the last days and establish His kingdom. Mount Zion will be consecrated to the Lord and all defilement removed. "Jacob" refers to the Southern Kingdom and "Joseph" the Northern Kingdom. They will be united into one nation and enter the Messianic Kingdom together, possessing the inheritance promised to them. It appears from Isaiah 11:10-16, a parallel passage, that Moab and Edom will be restored as nations in the last days, but the Jews will burn them as stubble (see Ex. 15:7; Isa. 10:17; Matt. 3:12 for parallels).

God will defeat your enemies (Obad. 19-20). Israel will

reclaim the land formerly inhabited by the Edomites (the Negev), the Philistines (the Shephelah), and the Samaritans (Ephraim). The Jews have been struggling to possess their inheritance for centuries, but other powers have always stood in the way. The Jews will "possess their possessions" without the help of any nation, but only through the help of the Lord their God. Israel has returned to their land in unbelief, and the nation was established in 1948. However, one day they shall see their Messiah and believe on Him, and the nation will be "born in a day" (Isa. 66:8; Zech. 12:10–13:1; 14:1-9).

God will establish the kingdom (Obad. 21). The Lord will reign from Mount Zion, where His temple will stand, "and all the nations will stream to it" (Isa. 2:2, NASB). It's interesting to note that King Messiah will have "deliverers" ("saviors" KJV) assist Him in His rule over the nations. This fact should be studied with reference to our Lord's promises to His apostles (Matt. 19:27-30) and those who are faithful to Him today (24:42-51; 25:14-30; Luke 19:11-27). Jesus teaches that faithfulness to Him today will mean reigning with Him in the kingdom.

All of God's children look forward to the day when the kingdoms of this world will become the kingdom of our Lord, and He shall reign forever and ever (Rev. 11:15). Then every knee shall bow to Him and every tongue confess that He is Lord of all.

Meanwhile, God's people must do all they can to get the Gospel out to the billions of people in this world who have never had the opportunity to hear the name of Jesus or learn how to trust Him and be saved. When the great and terrible Day of the Lord dawns, the nations of the world will be judged for the way they have treated one another and the nation of Israel. Until that day dawns, God's church must keep praying "Thy kingdom come" and seek to obey His command to take the Gospel to the whole world.

Micah in His Time

Micah's name is an abbreviated form of "Micaiah" and means "Who is like Jehovah?" (see 7:18) He was from the village of Moresheth near Gath, about twenty-five miles southwest of Jerusalem; and he prophesied during the last half of the eighth century B.C., during the reigns of Jotham (750–735), Ahaz (735–715) and Hezekiah (715–686). He was a contemporary of Isaiah (1:1) in Judah and Amos and Hosea (1:1) in Israel, the Northern Kingdom.

The death of King Uzziah in 739 was a watershed experience for Judah. During Jotham's reign, Assyria grew stronger; and when Ahaz ascended the throne, both Syria and Israel tried to pressure him into joining a rebellion against Assyria (Isa. 7). Jeremiah 26:18 informs us that it was the ministry of Micah that encouraged the great reformation in Judah under the leadership of King Hezekiah (2 Kings 18–20).

Society in Judah was rapidly changing from rural to urban. In defiance of the Law of Moses, wealthy investors were buying up small family farms and developing huge land holdings, which created serious problems for the poor. Having come from a farming community, Micah championed the oppressed poor and rebuked the "robber barons" for their selfishness. Amos echoed the same message.

Micah saw the coming judgment of the Northern Kingdom under Assyria (722) as well as the fall of Jerusalem and Judah under the Babylonians (606–596). He sought to call the Jews back to faithful worship of Jehovah and sincere obedience to His covenant, but they refused to listen. He pled for social justice and a concern for the helpless, but the people would not repent.

A Suggested Outline of the Book of Micah

Key idea: God judges sin and calls for justice
Key verse: Micah 6:8
Micah delivered three messages (Note "Hear" in 1:2; 3:1; 6:1)

I. A warning message: judgment is coming—1:1–2:13
   1. The Judge appears—1:1-5
   2. The nations are judged—1:6-16
      (1) Judgment on Samaria—1:6-9
      (2) Judgment on Judah—1:10-16
   3. Why judgment is coming—2:1-11
      (1) Because of covetousness—2:1-5
      (2) Because of false prophets—2:6-11
   4. Hope for the remnant—2:12-13

II. A promise message: a Deliverer is coming—3:1–5:15
   1. The sins of the leaders—3:1-12
   2. The future of the nation—4:1-13
   3. The coming of Messiah—5:1-5
   4. The defeat of the enemy—5:6-15

III. A challenge message: trust the Lord now—6:1–7:20
   1. In spite of the indictment—6:1-8
   2. In spite of the sentence—6:9–7:6
   3. Because of the Lord's mercies—7:7-20

EIGHT

Judgment Is Coming!

King David had a great many talented men in his army, but the most valuable were perhaps the men of Issachar, who had "understanding of the times, to know what Israel ought to do" (1 Chron. 12:32). Because they understood the times, the men of Issachar abandoned the ill-fated house of Saul and joined forces with David, God's chosen king. They saw which way God's hand was moving, and they obediently moved in that direction.

Micah of Moresheth was a man who had the same kind of discernment because God gave him insight into the changes taking place on the national and international scene. Micah received three messages from the Lord to deliver to the people in hopes they would abandon their idolatry and return to sincere faith in the Lord. (For the three messages, see the suggested outline of the Book of Micah.)

The first message (Micah 1:1–2:13) was a warning that divine judgment was coming on both Judah and Israel (Samaria). This message was fulfilled in 722 B.C. when Assyria defeated Israel, and in 606–586 when the Babylonians invaded Judah, destroyed Jerusalem and the temple, and took thousands of people captive to Babylon. When God's servant speaks, it pays to listen!

1. Declaration: God's wrath is coming (Micah 1:1-5)

When the Prophet Amos was about to indict Israel and Judah, he started by condemning the Gentile nations around them (Amos 1–2); but the Prophet Micah didn't take that approach. Without any formal introduction, he moved right into his message and sounded the alarm.

The court is convened (Micah 1:2). The image in verses 2-5 is that of a court of law, with God as the Judge and Judah and Samaria as the defendants. Micah addresses all the people of the earth because God is the Lord of the whole earth (4:23) and all the nations are accountable to Him. God is both judge and witness; He bears witness from His holy temple where His Law was kept in the ark of the covenant. A holy God must act in righteousness and judge sin.

The Judge arrives (Micah 1:3-4). Today when the judge enters the courtroom from his or her chamber, everybody in the courtroom rises—a symbol of the respect we have for the judge and the law that he or she represents. But no judge ever came to court in the manner described by Micah! The verb "to come forth" means "to come forth for battle." God opens the court and declares war!

A judge comes to court to see to it that justice is done, and he or she isn't allowed to take sides. But when God comes to judge the nations, He has all the evidence necessary and doesn't have to call any witnesses. God is angry at His people because of their sins. That's why His coming makes the earth split and the mountains melt so that the rock flows like melted wax or a waterfall.[1]

The Judge names the defendants (Micah 1:5). God points an accusing finger at His own people—Israel and Judah—as represented by their capital cities, Samaria and Jerusalem. After seeing what Assyria did to Israel in 722, the leaders of

Judah should have repented and turned to the Lord, but they didn't. In fact, during the reign of Hezekiah, the Assyrians plundered Judah and would have taken Jerusalem had not the Lord miraculously intervened (Isa. 36–37).

Both Judah and Israel were guilty of idolatry, which is really rebellion against the Lord. When the nation was divided after Solomon's death, the Northern Kingdom established its own religious system in competition with the Mosaic worship in the temple at Jerusalem. But the people of Judah had secretly begun to worship the false gods of Canaan; and their hearts were not true to Jehovah, even when they stood in the temple courts and offered their sacrifices (Isa. 1). To God, the temple had become like one of the "high places" in the hills around Jerusalem, where the Jews secretly worshiped idols and offered their sacrifices.

2. Lamentation: the cities shall be ruined (Micah 1:6-16)

The prophet responded to God's message by acting like a grieving man at a funeral (v. 8; 2 Sam. 15:30). He was genuinely burdened because of what would happen to his people if they didn't heed God's Word and turn from their sin.

The ruin of Samaria (Micah 1:6-9). The capital city of the Northern Kingdom was situated on a hill that overlooked a fertile valley. The Prophet Isaiah called the city "the crown of pride" with "glorious beauty" (Isa. 28:1) and predicted that God's judgment would destroy the city (vv. 2-4). The Assyrians would turn the beautiful city into a heap of rubble, and her idols wouldn't be able to protect the city from its enemies.

God destroyed the city and nation of Samaria because the people rebelled against His Word, and He destroyed the Samaritan temple because it housed a false religion that was nothing but religious prostitution. (Throughout the Old Testament, idolatry is compared to prostitution.) But God destroyed the temple in Jerusalem because the leaders had turned the true religion into a false worship of Jehovah and the gods of the nations. Jehovah is a jealous God who will not share worship or glory with another (Ex. 20:5; 34:14; Deut. 4:24; 5:9; 6:15). The covenant God made with His people at Sinai was like a marriage contract, and their breaking that covenant was like committing adultery or engaging in prostitution.[2]

The destruction of the city of Samaria was begun in 722 under Sargon II, ruler of Assyria, who ordered many of the citizens to be taken captive or killed. Then he imported people into the land from various nations he had conquered; and as Jews and Gentiles intermarried, the result was a mixed race that the Jews despised. Even in our Lord's day, the Jews had no dealings with the Samaritans (John 4:1-9).

The ruin of Judah (Micah 1:9-16). The problem with Samaria was that she was toxic; her infection had spread to Judah. The prophet wept over his land, the way you would weep over an incurable patient in the hospital (v. 9). Isaiah used a similar image to describe the plight of Judah (Isa. 1:5-6), and Jeremiah wept because the spiritual leaders in his day didn't deal drastically with the sin sickness of the people (Jer. 6:14; 7:8; 8:11).

Micah describes the ruin of the southern part of Judah (the Shephelah) by the invading Assyrians in 701 B.C. (Micah 1:10-16; see 2 Kings 18:7ff).[3] They swept through the land and took forty-six cities, but they could not take Jerusalem because God protected it. Micah used a series of puns based on the names of the cities and their similarity in sound to familiar Hebrew words. For example, "Gath" is similar to the Hebrew word for "tell." Thus he wrote, "Tell it not in Gath." Beth Ophrah means "house of dust." Thus he wrote, "Roll in the dust." The people of Shaphir ("pleasant, beautiful") would look neither beautiful nor pleasant as they were herded off as naked prisoners of war.

The roll call of cities goes on. The citizens of Zaanan ("come out") would not be able to come out because of the danger. Beth Ezel means "house of taking away," and the city would be taken away. Maroth is related to "mara/myrrh" and means "bitterness," and the city would experience bitter calamity ("writhe in pain," NIV). Since Lachish sounds like the Hebrew word for "a team of swift horses," he warned them to harness their horses to the chariots and try to escape.[4]

Micah came to his own city, Moresheth, which sounds like a Hebrew word meaning "betrothed"; and brides were given farewell gifts. In other words, the town would no longer belong to Judah but would "leave home" and belong to the invaders. Since Aczib means "deception," the connection is obvious; and Mareshah sounds like the word for "conqueror," and the town would be conquered by the enemy.

The tragedy of this successful invasion is that it need not have happened. Had the people of Israel and Judah turned to the Lord in repentance and faith, He would have given them glorious victory. Instead, they believed the false prophets, held fast to their idols, and sinned their way right into defeat. Sad to say, even the little children suffered and went into exile (1:16), all because of the sins of the parents.

3. Accusation: the sins of the people (Micah 2:1-11)

How could the Lord Jehovah permit such suffering and shame to come to His covenant people? Were they not His special heritage? Was not the land His love gift to them? *That was why He was punishing them!* "You only have I chosen of all the families of the earth; therefore I will punish you for all your sins" (Amos 3:2, NIV). Privilege brings responsibility, and responsibility brings accountability. The prophet held them accountable for two particular sins: covetousness (Micah 2:1-5) and listening to false prophets (vv. 6-11).

Covetousness (Micah 2:1-5). The Mosaic Law required that the land remain with the families and within the tribes. The land actually belonged to the Lord (Lev. 25:2, 23, 38), and He "leased" it to the people in return for their obedience to His law. If they disobeyed Him, they defiled the land and invited His judgment (18:24-30; Num. 35:33-34). If anybody sold family property, it was only until the next Year of Jubilee, at which time all land reverted back to the original owners (Lev. 25:13-17). This arrangement kept the rich from oppressing the poor and helped to stabilize the economy.

But the wealthy "robber barons" in Micah's day were bent on acquiring large estates on which they could enslave the poor and thus make huge profits with little investment. So intent were they on their pursuit of wealth that they made their ruthless plans in bed at night and then got up early the next morning to carry them out. Because of their wealth and their authority in the land, these men controlled the courts and the councils at the city gates. Thus they got what they wanted.

It mattered little to these proud men that they took away farms illegally and evicted families from their homes mercilessly. They practiced the world's version of The Golden Rule: "Whoever has the gold makes the rules." They forgot that the Lord owned the land, the Lord made the laws, and the Lord has compassion on the poor and the oppressed (Ex. 23:11; Lev. 25:25; Ps. 82:3; Prov. 21:13; Jer. 22:16). But even if these thieves had no fear of God, they should have had concern for their fellow human beings and treated them like people made in the image of God.

The name for this sin is "materialism," and it's committed by people who are covetous and obsessed with acquiring more and more wealth and "things." But "robber barons" aren't the only people who commit these sins. Parents rob their children of time and companionship by working at several jobs so they can make more money to buy more "fun."

People rob God of tithes and offerings that are rightfully His just so they can enjoy "the good life" (Mal. 3:7-12). People forget Matthew 6:33 and put everything else ahead of the kingdom of God.

However, ultimately the covetous sinners Micah addressed would reap what they sowed; and the dreadful harvest of their sins would one day appear (Micah 2:3-5). Their proud self-confidence would be taken from them, their authority would be gone, their crooked accomplices would turn against them and laugh at them, and their vast holdings would be snatched from their hands. They would see everything they lived for and sinned to acquire be taken over by the enemy and wasted. Many of them would go into exile and die away from the land they had coveted and stolen from innocent people.

False prophets (Micah 2:6-11). Just as the false prophets attacked Jeremiah (5:31) and Amos (7:10-17) for preaching God's truth, so the false prophets attacked Micah for faithfully declaring the message of God. These men espoused a shallow theology that had no place for either sin or repentance. "We are God's special people," they argued, "and He would never permit these judgments to happen in the land." As long as the people participated in religious services, they would never incur the wrath of God, even if their hearts were not in their worship. The Jews were Abraham's children, and God would never break the promises He made to Abraham. Such were their false premises.

What these counterfeit religious leaders forgot was that God's covenants involve precepts as well as promises, obligations as well as blessings. Merely going through the motions of religion isn't the same as worshiping God "in spirit and in truth" (John 4:23). Anybody can join the crowd and be a part of some popular religious movement; but it takes devotion, prayer, obedience, and submission to worship God "with reverence and godly fear" (Heb. 12:28, NKJV). "Popular religion" is usually false religion, for the road to life is narrow and lonely (Matt. 7:13-20) and those who walk it are invariably persecuted (2 Tim. 3:12).

It is God who speaks in Micah 2:7b-13 as He defends His faithful servant. The fact that these religious leaders rejected Micah's message didn't mean the message was wrong; it meant that the hearers were wrong. The way we respond to God's Word indicates our relationship to the Lord. "He who is of God hears God's words; therefore you do not hear, because you are not of God" (John 8:47, NKJV).

These false prophets were deceiving and robbing the people by giving them false assurance that everything was well in the land. God pictured their sinful deeds by describing two carefree men—a rich man walking confidently down the street and a victorious soldier returning home with the spoils of the battle—and both of them are robbed! Because of the evil rich leaders, the confident mother and her family find themselves thrust from their homes and robbed of their land.

God originally gave the Jewish people the land of Canaan to be their "rest" from the trials of the wilderness wanderings (Deut. 12:9-10; Josh. 22:4; 23:1). After they had conquered the land and claimed their tribal inheritance, they should have enjoyed rest and blessing in the land, but instead they turned to the idols of the surrounding nations and rebelled against God. God punished them in their land by bringing in different nations that robbed and enslaved them (see the Book of Judges). But the nation didn't learn from its history; the people repeated the same sins as their ancestors *but thought they would avoid the same consequences.* Since they had defiled the land, God removed them from it.

Micah urged the people to get out of the land because no rest would be found there, in spite of what the false prophets promised. These men would preach any message the people wanted to hear, just so long as they were provided with their strong drink! The false prophets were using religion to make money and enjoy pleasure, and they had no concern for the future of the nation.

4. Consolation: hope for the future (Micah 2:12-13)

The faithful prophet must expose sin and announce judgment, but he must also provide consolation and hope for those who receive his message and turn to God. Consolation without true repentance is only giving a false hope; it's saying "Peace, peace!" when there is no peace. But conviction without hope creates only hopelessness, like performing surgery without providing healing.

The Lord seems to be speaking here to the entire nation ("all of you, O Jacob . . . Israel," NIV), and His promise seems to reach ahead to the end times when Israel and Judah will be united and their King Messiah will reign over them. Micah describes a triumphant procession into the land, with King Messiah at the head and the Lord leading the people, just as He had when they had left Egypt (v. 13).

However, until that glorious day, God will deal with the "remnant" of His people. The "remnant" is a very important doctrine in the prophetic books, and there are many references to it.[5] Though the nation of Israel might rebel against God, there would always be a faithful remnant that would trust Him and seek to do His will; and God would work because of the faith of this remnant. (This is also true of the professing church.) The hope of the nation lies with the remnant.

A weak and weary remnant returned to Judah after the Babylonian Captivity, but it never became the great nation that the prophets promised. That will happen when the Lord returns, claims His chosen nation, and establishes His kingdom. The Messiah is described in verse 13 as "One who breaks open the way" (NIV), that is, who opens the doors that confine the Jews in the various nations so that He might bring them to their land. God certainly did this when the exiles left Babylon, but the promise here is for the last days when the Messiah shall come to overcome His enemies and redeem His chosen people.

Micah's first message aroused the opposition of the false prophets, but it didn't change the hearts of the people. Thus he gave a second message, announcing that "the Deliverer is coming."

But we today need to deal with our sins of covetousness, selfishness, and willingness to believe "religious lies." We must abandon "soft religion" that pampers our pride and makes it easy for us to sin. Why? Because "our God is a consuming fire" (Heb. 12:29), and "The Lord shall judge His people" (10:30). Remember, judgment begins in the house of the Lord (1 Peter 4:17).

N I N E

A Ruler Is Coming!

Micah's second message is at the heart of the book and focuses on Israel's future. First, Micah rebuked the leaders of the nation for their sinful conduct, which God would judge (3:1-12), and then he outlined the events that would usher in the promised kingdom (4:1–5:15). Knowing that God has such a glorious future planned for their nation should have motivated the leaders to turn from their sins and obey the Lord. "Everyone who has this hope in him purifies himself, just as He is pure" (1 John 3:3, NIV). Alas, they didn't even pay attention to the sermon!

1. Rebuke: the sins of the leaders (Micah 3:1-12)
As with Micah's other two messages, this second message opens with a call for the people to "hear" what the Lord would say through His servant (1:2; 6:1). It's as though Micah had shouted, "Listen! God is speaking! This is important!" The statement reminds us of our Lord's repeated admonition, "Who has ears to hear, let him hear!" or the warning in Hebrews 12:25: "See that you do not refuse Him who speaks" (NKJV).

It's a dangerous thing to turn a deaf ear to the voice of God when He speaks through His Word. "Today, if you will hear His voice, do not harden your hearts" (3:7-8, NKJV). All creation responds to the voice of God and gladly obeys His will *except man made in God's image!* Yet the Father lovingly says to us, "Now therefore, listen to Me, My children; pay attention to the words of My mouth" (Prov. 7:24, NKJV).

Micah opened his message by rebuking the *civil authorities in the land (Micah 3:1-4),* men who were not only permitting the wealthy to exploit the poor but were also doing it themselves! Leaders are supposed to love the good and hate the evil, but these men were just the opposite: They "hate the good, and love the evil" (v. 2). Ideal leaders are described as "able men, such as fear God, men of truth, hating covetousness" (Ex. 18:21, NKJV). Micah's fellow Prophet Amos wrote, "Seek good and not evil, that you may live. . . . Hate evil, love good; establish justice in the gate" (Amos 5:14-15, NKJV; see Prov. 8:13). The city gate, of course, was the place where the elders met to settle disputes and make official decisions (Ruth 4:1ff). If there was no justice in the cities, there could be no justice in the land.

The description of these rulers' actions reminds you more of ravenous beasts than of human beings. Instead of being faithful shepherds who protected the flock (Micah 2:12; 7:14), they attacked the sheep, skinned them alive, butchered them, chopped them up, and made stew out of them! But the day would come when these wolves in shepherds' clothing would cry out for God's mercy, but no mercy would be given. "Then My anger shall be kindled against them in that day, and I will forsake them, and I will hide My face from them, and they shall be devoured" (Deut. 31:17).

Micah then turned to rebuke *the false prophets (Micah 3:5-8),* whose lies made it easy for the corrupt officials to carry on their evil deeds. "A wonderful and horrible thing is committed in the land; the prophets prophesy falsely, and the priests bear rule by their means; and My people love to have it so" (Jer. 5:30-31). When God is left out of human government, it's easy for officials to use their authority selfishly to exploit the people.

As long as you gave them something to eat and drink (Micah 2:11), the prophets would declare whatever kind of message you wanted to hear. Like the false prophets in Jeremiah's day, they announced peace when war and desolation were just around the corner (Jer. 6:13-14; 8:10-11). But the time would come when these men who claimed to see the light would be shrouded in darkness, and everybody would know that they were counterfeits. They would cry out to the Lord, but He would not answer.

God's true prophet is described in Micah 3:8: This prophet is filled with the Spirit, faithfully proclaiming God's message and unafraid of what people might say or do. Micah fearlessly told the people their sins and warned them that judgment was coming, while the false prophets tickled the people's ears and told them what they wanted to hear.

Few men are as pitiable as those who claim to have a call from God but who tailor their sermons to please the people. Their first rule is "Don't rock the boat"; and their second is "Give the people what they want." But a true servant of God declares God's message regardless of whether people like it or not. He'd like to be a peacemaker, but sometimes he has to be a troublemaker. No wonder Jeremiah cried out, "Alas, my mother, that you gave me birth, a man with whom the whole land strives and contends!" (Jer. 15:10, NIV)

Micah also addressed *all the leaders of the land (Micah 3:9-12)*—the rulers, the priests, and the prophets—and accused them of numerous sins: committing injustice, distorting the truth, murdering innocent people, accepting bribes, and while doing these evil deeds, claiming to be serving the Lord! "We are depending on the Lord," they said. "Is He not among us? Then nothing evil can happen to us." It was hypocrisy of the worst kind.

Their ignorance of the Lord's character and the terms of His covenant gave them this false confidence. "Since we're Jews," they reasoned, "God's chosen people and sharers in His covenant, the Lord will never permit anything evil to happen to us. Even if we sin, He will never abandon us to the enemy." Their thinking was not unlike that of people today who "profess that they know God; but in works they deny Him" (Titus 1:16).

Any theology that makes it easy for us to sin is not biblical theology. Had the rulers, prophets, and priests read and pondered Leviticus 26 and Deuteronomy 28–30, they would have discovered that the God of the covenant is a holy God who will not countenance high-handed sin. They would also have learned that the blessings of the covenant depended on their obeying the conditions of the covenant, and that God punishes His people when they disobey.

What would be the result of the leaders' flouting God's law? Their holy city and temple would be destroyed, and thousands of Jewish people would be exiled to Babylon (Micah 4:10). God would rather destroy the city and the beautiful temple than allow His people to defile His property by their sins. The destruction of Jerusalem in 606–586 is a reminder to God's people that when God says, "Be holy, for I am holy,"[1] *He really means it!*

"For the sins of her prophets, and the iniquities of her priests" (Lam. 4:13) the nation was defeated and the city and temple were destroyed. That's why the prophet opened his message by rebuking the spiritual leaders of the land, not the unbelievers. If Micah were ministering among us today, he would probably visit denominational offices, pastors' conferences, Bible colleges, and seminaries to warn Christian leaders that privilege brings responsibility and responsibility brings accountability.

2. Hope: the promises of the Lord (Micah 4:1–5:5a)[2]

Micah moved from the destruction of Jerusalem (606–586) to "the last days" when there will be a new Jerusalem and a rebuilt temple at the heart of the righteous kingdom of Messiah. The period known as "the last days" began with the ministry of Christ (Heb. 1:1-2) and will climax with His return to establish His kingdom on earth. The Lord gave His people four wonderful promises.

A promised kingdom (Micah 4:1-8).[3] The situation of the two little Jewish kingdoms was hopeless when Micah delivered his messages. Assyria was about to pounce on Israel and put an end to that nation, and then the Assyrian army would ravage Judah and almost take Jerusalem. When the outlook is grim, try the uplook. Thus the prophet encouraged the people to look ahead to what God had promised for His chosen people.

God promised that the nation would be united and the people returned to their land. Jerusalem would become the world's most important city, the temple would be rebuilt, and the true worship of Jehovah would be restored[4] (see Ezek. 40–48). Instead of the Gentile nations fighting the Jews, they would "stream" to Jerusalem to worship God and hear His Word. There would be peace among the nations because they would obey God's truth, submit to the Messiah's rule, and destroy their instruments of war.[5]

Every Jewish family wanted to achieve what Micah described in 4:4: a pleasant home with a productive garden in a peaceful land (see 1 Kings 4:25; Isa. 36:16). But even more than peace and economic stability was the blessing of knowing the Lord and obeying Him (Micah 4:5). This verse doesn't refer to the future, because during the Kingdom Age all the nations will worship Jehovah. It was an affirmation of faith on the part of the true believers, the remnant in the land: "The other nations may now be serving their own gods, which are false gods; but we will walk in the name of Jehovah, the true God, and obey Him alone."

Though the remnant of Jews might be small, weak, and lame, God will gather them from all the nations and make a mighty army out of them (vv. 6-7a). Messiah will rule over them, and Jerusalem will become the glorious capital city for His kingdom. Jerusalem had once been David's capital city, the shepherd-king who cared for the flock (Ps. 78:67-72), but after the death of Josiah, not one of his four successors was a godly man. Messiah, the Son of David, will one day reign from Jerusalem and care for His flock as a faithful Shepherd-King.

A promised deliverance (Micah 4:9-10). The city of Jerusalem is called "daughter of Zion" (cities are usually classified as feminine), a term of endearment that assured the people of God's loving care no matter what might happen. But the city was in travail, like a woman with child, because the enemy had arrived and was capturing the people and taking them to Babylon. However, the exile wasn't the end; for God will redeem a remnant and bring them back to the land.

Had the leaders listened to the Prophet Jeremiah and peacefully surrendered to the Babylonians, they would have saved the city and the temple, but they resisted God's will, and their city and temple were ruined. However, Jeremiah promised that the exile would last only seventy years, and then the remnant could return and rebuild the city and the temple.

A promised conquest (Micah 4:11-13). Once again, the prophet looked down the centuries to the end times and saw his people being attacked by many Gentile nations, all of them gloating over Israel because they are so sure of defeating the Jews (see Zech. 12:1-9; 14:1-11). The nations are sure of victory because they ignore Scripture and don't know

God's plans for His people (Jer. 29:11).

Israel will look weak and defenseless, but the Lord will make their soldiers sharp threshing instruments to "harvest" the nations (Rev. 14:14-20). God will give them "horns" (a symbol of power) and "hoofs" so that they will have both power and speed as they attack their enemies. This great battle is usually called "the battle of Armageddon," although that phrase is not found in Scripture (Rev. 16:16; 19:17-21). When the battle is over, the victorious Jewish army will devote all the spoils to the service of the Lord.

A promised King (Micah 5:1-5a). Now Micah looks ahead to the Babylonian siege of Jerusalem. So many soldiers are encamped around Jerusalem that Micah calls her "the city [daughter] of troops." When King Zedekiah and his officers see that their situation is hopeless, they try to escape, but the Babylonians catch up with them and capture them (2 Kings 25:1-7). Of course, they humiliate the king by striking him with a rod across his face.[6] Then they kill his sons, put out his eyes, bind him, and take him to Babylon.

The fact that Micah 5:2 is in contrast to verse 1 ("But thou, Bethlehem") is another proof that verse 1 is not speaking about Jesus; for verses 2-5 definitely refer to Messiah. God selected "the little town of Bethlehem" as the place where the King of the Jews was to be born. It was this prophecy that the priests shared with the magi who came to Jerusalem looking for the King (Matt. 2:1-12).

Bethlehem ("house of bread") has an interesting history. Jacob's favorite wife, Rachel, died near Bethlehem when she gave birth to Benjamin, and she was buried nearby (Gen. 35:16-20). Matthew cites this when he reports the slaying of the innocent children by Herod (Matt. 2:16-18; see Jer. 31:15). In her pain, Rachel named her son Ben-oni, which means "son of my sorrow"; but Jacob renamed the boy, calling him Benjamin, "son of my right hand." These two names remind us of our Lord's suffering and glory, the cross and the throne at the Father's right hand.

Ruth and Naomi came to Bethlehem, and there Boaz fell in love with Ruth and married her. Ruth is an ancestress of the Messiah (Matt. 1:3). Of course, David was Bethlehem's greatest son; and it was through David's family that the promised Messiah would be born (2 Sam. 7; Matt. 1:1; Luke 1:26-27; Rom. 1:3). The Jews knew that their Messiah would come from Bethlehem (John 7:42).

In this prophecy, Micah reveals a number of important facts about the Messiah. To begin with, He is eternal God, for His "goings out are from old . . . from days of eternity" (see NIV margin). Jesus stepped out of eternity into human history, sent by the Father to die for the sins of the world (1 John 4:14). But He is also truly man, for He is born as a human child. We have here the miracle of the Incarnation (John 1:14).

You would think that the very Son of God would come to a great city like Athens or Jerusalem, but He chose to be born in a humble stable (or cave) in Bethlehem. However, the day would come when He would be glorified and take His throne in heaven; and one day, He shall return to be Ruler over His people.

However, before He can stand as a Shepherd and care for His flock, His own people must reject Him. Between the cross and the Kingdom Age, Israel will be "given up" by the Lord until the time when Jesus returns and the nation is "born" into her kingdom (see Isa. 66:8). This King will reign to the ends of the earth and will bring peace to all nations. Today, of course, Christ gives peace to all who will come to Him by faith (Matt. 11:28-30; Rom. 5:1).

Micah presented an encouraging scenario to the people, but they didn't seem to grasp its significance; for if they had, they would have turned to the Lord in gratitude and repentance. Whenever a prophet foretold the future, it was to awaken the people to their responsibilities in the present. Bible prophecy isn't entertainment for the curious; it's encouragement for the serious.

3. Victory: the purging of the nation (Micah 5:5b-15)
As he continued to view the distant scene, Micah announced that Israel's future enemies would be defeated (vv. 5b-6), the Jewish remnant would be blessed (vv. 7-9), and the nation would be purged of its sins (vv. 10-15).

The enemy defeated (Micah 5:5b-6). "The Assyrian" named in verse 5 isn't the Assyrian army of Micah's day, for the Jews in that day certainly didn't defeat Assyria and rule over her land. The Assyrians soundly defeated Israel, and the land of Israel was ruined. "The Assyrian" is another way of saying "the enemy," and here it refers to Israel's enemies in the last days when all nations will gather against her (Zech. 10:10-11; 12:9; 14:1-3).

The phrase "seven shepherds . . . eight leaders" is a way of saying "many shepherds, many leaders," and is similar to the repeated statement of Amos "for three transgressions . . . and for four" (Amos 1:3, 6, 9, etc.). When the enemy attacks in the last days, God will raise up leaders to face the enemy, just as He had raised up the judges and heroes like David. But Micah makes it clear that God is the Deliverer who will enable Israel to defeat her enemies and rule over their lands. The "he" of Micah 5:6 is the "ruler" of verse 2.

The remnant blessed (Micah 5:7-9). Though small in number, the Jewish remnant of the last days will experience great help from the Lord as they face their enemies. Micah used two similes to illustrate this blessing: the refreshing dew from heaven and the conquering strength of the lion. God will enable His people to overcome like lions and then bring fruitfulness to the world like the dew that watered Israel's crops (Ps. 133:3). Israel will triumph over her enemies through the power of the Lord.

The nation purged (Micah 5:10-15). In Micah's day, both Israel and Judah were guilty of sins that violated God's law and grieved God's heart. Time after time, He had sent messengers to the people to denounce their sins and warn of impending judgment, but the people wouldn't listen (2 Chron. 36:14-21). In the last days, Israel will return to her land in unbelief and practice these same sins. But God will purge the land and prepare them for a new life in the kingdom. They will see their Messiah, trust Him, and be saved (Zech. 12:10–13:1).

God will destroy all their military defenses, the things that they trusted, instead of trusting the Lord. He will end their traffic with demonic powers and eliminate all idolatry from the land (Zech. 13:2). Israel will now seek to please God and obey His law and not imitate the sins of the nations on which God will "take vengeance."

God has not cast aside His people (Rom. 11:1); for today, there is a believing remnant of Jews in the church. One day, God will gather the unbelieving Jewish nation to their land, cause them to experience great suffering, and then reveal Himself to them and give birth to a new nation. The prophets saw that day and tried to convey its message to the people of their day, but they wouldn't listen.

Christians today look for Jesus to return to gather His people to Himself (1 Thes. 4:13-18) and then establish His righteous kingdom. Peter assures us that "the Day of the Lord will come as a thief in the night"; and then, in light of this fact, he asks, "Therefore . . . what manner of persons ought you to be in holy conduct and godliness?" (2 Peter 3:10, 11, NKJV) Future hope ought to produce present holiness.

Are we ready for His return?

T E N

MICAH 6-7

"Thy Kingdom Come"

The prophet has delivered two of his three messages: a message of warning (1–2) and a message of promise (3–5). His third message was a challenge for them to trust the Lord and obey His will, for only then could the nation escape terrible punishment and fulfill God's purposes in this world.

As you read Old Testament history and prophecy, keep in mind how important it was for Israel to be obedient to the Lord. God had raised up the nation to bring blessing *to the whole world (Gen. 12:1-3)*, for it was through Israel that the Savior would come. "Salvation is of the Jews" (John 4:22). When the Jews began to adopt the practices of the godless nations around them, it defiled them and made them less able to do the work God had called them to do. It was because they despised their high and holy calling that the nation had to be chastened so severely.

Micah's first message was presented as a courtroom drama, and so was this third message. The Judge declared the indictment (Micah 6:1-8), pronounced the sentence (6:9–7:6) and then *graciously promised mercy (7:7-20)!* Micah used these three factors—guilt, punishment, and mercy—as arguments to plead with his people to repent and return to the Lord. "Trust the Lord, not in spite of these things but *because of these things!*" is his closing message; and it's a message we need to hear today.

1. Because of great guilt, trust the Lord (Micah 6:1-8)

The sins of the people were hidden behind a veneer of religious activity—routine worship that didn't come from their hearts. Micah's contemporary, the Prophet Isaiah, told the people that the nation was sick from head to foot (Isa. 1:5-6) but wouldn't admit it, and that their "worship" was nothing more than "trampling" the temple courts (v. 12). They were like the patient who asked the doctor to retouch his X rays so he wouldn't have to endure surgery! His deceit didn't cure him; it made him worse.

In this courtroom scene, *the Lord called the witnesses (Micah 6:1-2)* and told the people to be prepared to plead their case. The Lord opened the proceedings by telling His side of the controversy, emphasizing the gracious way He had dealt with the nation from the very beginning. He redeemed them from Egyptian slavery; He gave them leaders who guided them through the wilderness with His help; and He brought them to their promised inheritance. Of course, throughout this journey, the Lord had put up with their unbelief, disobedience, and repeated complaining (Ps. 106).

On three occasions, Balak, king of Moab, commanded Balaam to curse Israel, but God turned the curse into blessing (Num. 22–24; Deut. 23:5; Neh. 13:2). The Israelites didn't even know that this spiritual battle was going on; yet God protected His people. What did the Jews do in return? They became friendly with the Moabites, attended their idolatrous religious rites, and committed fornication with their women! (see Num. 25). What Balaam couldn't do by means of his curses, the Jews themselves did with their sinful lusts.

The phrase "from Shittim unto Gilgal" (Micah 6:5)

reminded the people of Israel's crossing of the Jordan River and entering the Promised Land (Josh. 3–4). The same God who opened and closed the Red Sea also opened and closed the Jordan River so His people might claim their inheritance. He did for them what they couldn't do for themselves, but they didn't remember.

It's good for God's people to know the past and remember with gratitude all that God has done for them. The word "remember" is found at least fourteen times in the Book of Deuteronomy, and frequently the Jews were instructed to teach their children the mighty deeds of the Lord (Ex. 10:2; 13:8, 14; Deut. 6:20ff; Josh. 22:24; Ps. 78:1-8).

While we shouldn't live in the past, we must learn from the past, or we'll commit the same mistakes of the past. As philosopher George Santayana wrote, "Those who cannot remember the past are condemned to repeat it." Because Israel forgot God's mercies (Ps. 106:7), they also ignored God's commandments. The result was a hard heart that deliberately rebelled against God's will. God had every right to ask them, "What have I done to you that you should treat Me this way?"

Now *the people replied to God (Micah 6:6-7).* Instead of confessing their sins or standing mute because their mouths had been shut by their sense of guilt (Rom. 3:19), they asked what they could do to get rid of their sins. Their request shows how shallow their spiritual life really was and that they were ignorant of the enormity of their sin and the high cost of forgiveness. They were like the rich young ruler who didn't really see himself as a condemned sinner before God (Mark 10:17-27), but they were not like the people at Pentecost who were cut to the heart and cried out, "What shall we do?" (Acts 2:37)

We get the impression that these questioners were interested in bargaining with God and "buying Him off," for they kept raising the bid. "Shall we bring a few calves as burnt offerings? If that's not enough, maybe we could offer a thousand sacrifices, such as Solomon offered [1 Kings 3:4; 8:63]? Would rivers of oil please Him? How about the ultimate sacrifice: our own flesh and blood offered on the altar, as Abraham did with Isaac?" But God doesn't bargain with sinners, and none of the sacrifices they offered to bring could have cleansed them from their sins.

"Doing penance" without truly repenting and trusting God's mercy only multiplies the sin and deadens the conscience. Thinking they were good enough to please God, the people asked Jesus, "What shall we do, that we may work the works of God?" He replied, "This is the work of God, that you believe in Him whom He sent" (John 6:28-29, NKJV). True saving faith comes from a heart that's been broken in repentance and realizes that no amount of good works can atone for sin (Acts 20:21; 26:20; Eph. 2:8-9).

The prophet spoke to the people (Micah 6:8) and told them exactly what the Lord wanted each of them to do. It was a personal matter that each individual sinner had to consider. His reply emphasized moral and ethical conduct, not religious ceremonies.[1] Of course, we can't "do justly" unless we've been justified by faith and are right with God (Ps. 32:1-2; Rom. 4:1-8). And how can we "love mercy" if we've not personally experienced God's mercy? (Eph. 2:4; Titus 3:5) If we want to "walk humbly with [our] God," we must first bow humbly before Him, confess our sins, and claim His promise of forgiveness (Luke 14:11; James 4:10).

Our Lord's parable about the Pharisee and publican in the temple (Luke 18:9-14) illustrates all three points. The publican was justified by faith, not by doing the kind of good works that the Pharisee boasted about. Since the publican depended on God's mercy to save him, he humbled himself before the Lord. The Pharisee, on the other hand, informed

God (and whoever was listening in the temple) how good he was and therefore how much he deserved eternal life.

To make Micah 6:8 a salvation text is to misunderstand what the prophet was saying to God's disobedient covenant people. None of us can do what God requires until first we come to God as broken sinners who need to be saved. Unsaved people who think they are doing justly, loving mercy, and walking humbly with God are only fooling themselves, no matter how moral their lives may be. "Not by works of righteousness which we have done, but according to His mercy He saved us" (Titus 3:5).

The people to whom Micah ministered simply didn't get the point of his messages. The very fact that they were so guilty before God should have motivated them to turn from their shallow religion, humble themselves, and seek God's mercy. The only people God can save are lost people; the only people God can forgive are guilty people. If we see ourselves as God sees us, then we can by faith become what He wants us to become.

2. Because of impending judgment, trust the Lord (Micah 6:9–7:7)

For the second time in this message, Micah cried out to the people, "Listen!" (vv. 1, 9, NIV) Like the crowds that Jesus taught, these Jews had ears to hear His words, but they couldn't hear God's truth in those words (Matt. 13:9, 43). They lacked spiritual discernment.

God speaks about sin and its consequences (Micah 6:9-16). The Lord called to the people of Jerusalem to fear His name and heed what He had to say; for without the fear of the Lord, they could have neither knowledge nor wisdom (Prov. 1:7).[2] God specifically condemned the merchants of the city for being deceptive in their business practices (Micah 6:10-12). They used weights and measures that were dishonest so that customers didn't get full value for their money (see Lev. 19:35-36; Deut. 25:13-16).

Why did this sin grieve the Lord so much? Because by doing these illegal things, the businessmen were exploiting and abusing the poor and needy in the land for whom God has a special concern (Amos 8:4-10). The Mosaic economic system provided for the care of the poor and needy, but the wealthy merchants in Micah's time had abandoned the system. They robbed the poor of both justice and the necessities of life, a sin God could not overlook.

Moreover, along with making their own weights and measures and bribing the courts, the rich were openly violent (Micah 6:12; also see 2:2; 3:1-3). They forcibly evicted people from their houses and lands and left them helpless, without homes or any source of income. When the poor tried to protect themselves through the courts, the rich merchants lied about the situation and convinced the officials that their actions were right.

But God has ordained that people reap what they sow, whether good or evil (Hosea 8:7; Gal. 6:7-8). Therefore, judgment had to fall on the "robber barons" of the land. Indeed, God warned about two different kinds of judgments (Micah 6:13-16). The first (vv. 13-15) was already in progress, slow and secret, but very thorough. "Therefore, I have begun to destroy you, to ruin you because of your sins" (v. 13, NIV). This judgment was the collapse of their economic system, including their crops (stolen farms), their investments (stolen money), and even their enjoyment of all that they had accumulated. Everything these merchant thieves had amassed for their pleasure would disappear, and whatever they tried to enjoy would bring them no pleasure at all. (See God's covenant warnings in Deut. 28:15ff.)

The second judgment (Micah 6:16) would be sudden and open: the total ruin of the nation by the hand of Babylon.

That Micah should point to Babylon as the aggressor (4:10) is remarkable, because Babylon wasn't a major power on the international scene at that time. It was Assyria that everybody feared, and Assyria did ruin the Northern Kingdom in 722 and did do great damage to Judah in 701. But by the time Babylon was finished with Judah and Jerusalem, the nation would be in ruin and the people in derision. The people's sins found them out.

The Lord tried to use the judgment on the Northern Kingdom to awaken and warn the people of Judah, the Southern Kingdom, but they wouldn't listen. Their defense was "It can't happen here. We have the temple!" But they weren't obeying God's law or honoring His house. Instead, they were following the godless ways of two kings of Israel, Omri and Ahab, both of whom "did evil in the eyes of the Lord, and did worse than all who were before [them]" (1 Kings 16:25; see v. 30, NKJV). They should have followed the godly ways of King David, because it was for David's sake that God held back His judgment for so long (11:13, 32, 34, 36; 15:4).

The prophet speaks of his sorrow (Micah 7:1-7). The prophets not only declared God's message with their lips, but they also felt the burden of the people on their hearts. Jeremiah wept over the sins of the nation in his day and wished he could weep even more (Jer. 9:1ff), and Micah lamented because there were no godly people left in the land. Looking for a godly person was as futile as looking for summer fruit after the harvest was over.[3]

Micah compared the evil officials to hunters who wove clever nets and threw them over the helpless and trapped them. These officials and judges were skilled at weaving their nets (perverting the law so they could rob the unwary), but they weren't skilled at obeying God's laws. They were like briars and thorns that hurt people, when they should have been like concerned shepherds who helped people.

"The day of your watchmen" refers to the day of judgment when the watchmen on the walls would see the enemy approaching and call out to warn the people. God's prophets were His watchmen (Ezek. 3:18-21), constantly warning the nation, but the leaders wouldn't listen. They preferred lies to truth and this brought about a "time of . . . confusion" (Micah 7:4, NIV).

This confusion reached into every level of society. Not only was Micah grieved at the corruption of the officials, but also he was grieved at the unfaithfulness of the common people of the land (vv. 5-6). You couldn't trust anybody! When truth is no longer the standard for society, then everything starts to fall apart; for faithfulness to our word is the cement that holds society together. It had come to the place where neighbor couldn't trust neighbor, friend couldn't trust friend, and husbands and wives couldn't even trust each other. The basic unit of Jewish society, the family, was quickly falling apart. (In fact, Jesus quoted Micah 7:6 in Matt. 10:36.)

In the light of the terrible condition of the land and the judgment that was impending, wouldn't it have been a wise thing for the people to turn from their sin and trust the Lord? Would it not have been a smart thing for them to claim 2 Chronicles 7:14 and seek God's face so that He might heal their land? But sinners don't do wise things, because their eyes are blinded as they walk in the darkness (John 3:19-21).

3. Because of God's great mercies, trust the Lord (Micah 7:7-20)

The prophet reached a turning point when he looked away from the sins of the people and meditated on the faithfulness of the Lord. "But as for me, I watch in hope for the Lord, I wait for God my Savior; my God will hear me" (v. 7, NIV). He would "watch and pray" and put his trust only in the Lord. This verse is the "bridge" that connects the sections on sin and judgment with this closing section on hope.

In this final section of Micah's third message, we must distinguish several voices: the nation (vv. 8-10), the prophet (vv. 11-13), the Lord (vv. 14-15), and the prophet again (vv. 16-20). We must also realize that Micah is looking down through the centuries with prophetic vision to the time when Israel will come through great tribulation and enter into the promised kingdom. The Assyrian and Babylonian conquests were only foretastes of the tribulation to come, "dress rehearsals" as it were. But the future will bring victory to God's people, not defeat, when the Lord fulfills His promises and establishes the kingdom.

The voice of the nation (Micah 7:8-10). Perhaps the prophet is speaking on behalf of the remnant as he expresses their faith and courage. The enemy gloated over the defeated Jews and asked in derision, "Where is the Lord your God?" (v. 10, NIV; see Pss. 42:3, 10; 79:10; 115:2)[4] But the people trust God and have confidence that, though they had fallen, they would rise; though they were in darkness, they would see light; and though they had been defeated, they would eventually conquer their enemies and trample them like mud in the streets.

Since these events did not occur after the Assyrian and Babylonian invasions, they must be assigned to a future time. According to Jesus, the Jewish nation will experience great tribulation and become the target of all the Gentile nations in the end times (Matt. 24:15-31). In the end, however, Christ will return and give His people great victory.

The voice of the prophet (Micah 7:11-14). Micah speaks to the city of Jerusalem and assures her that, though she had been attacked and destroyed, she would one day be rebuilt. The prophets speak in glowing terms of Israel having a new city and temple (Isa. 2:1-5; Ezek. 40–48). Not only that, but also the boundaries of the nation would be expanded to include more territory than she had before.

In the light of this great promise, the prophet lifted his heart to the Lord in prayer (Micah 7:14) and asked Him to be the faithful Shepherd of Israel and care for His people (see 5:4; Isa. 40:11; Ps. 80:1). Micah longed for "the good old days" when the land was fruitful and peaceful and the people were like obedient sheep who followed their Shepherd.

The voice of the Lord (Micah 7:15). God replied to His faithful servant and assured him that He would indeed watch over His flock and care for them, just as He had when they had departed from the land of Egypt. The "exodus" image is sometimes used in Scripture to point to the "exodus" of the Jews in the end times from the nations of the world to their own land (Isa. 11:15-12:6; 35:8-10; 43:14-20; 51:9-11). God will perform great wonders for His people at a time in their history when the nations are united against them.

The voice of the prophet (Micah 7:16-20). When Israel departed from Egypt and God opened the sea, the other nations heard about it and feared (Ex. 15:14-16; Josh. 2:8-11). But the wonders the Lord will do for Israel in the last days will startle the nations even more. The Gentiles will see the power of God and be ashamed and unable to act. They will "hit the dust" like serpents and be humiliated. They will come out of their hiding places to submit to the Lord. It will mean total victory for Israel.

But the most important event will not be Israel's victory over her enemies but God's victory over Israel. The prophet was confident of the unchanging character of God. "Who is a God like You?" (Micah 7:18, NIV) reminds us of the meaning of Micah's name, "Who is like the Lord?" He is a God who pardons sin, forgives transgressions, and delights in showing mercy. He shows compassion to His people and deals with their sins with finality. Some students see Israel's exodus experience illustrated in verse 19: The Egyptian army was buried in the depths of the Red Sea and ended up in the mire.

Micah knew that God would not go back on His promises or His covenant agreements with His people. The people weren't always true to Jehovah, but He will be true to His people (2 Tim. 2:12-13). What He promised to Abraham, the father of the nation, He will fulfill in his many descendants. Micah could have sung

> How firm a foundation, ye saints of the Lord,
> Is laid for your faith in His excellent Word.

In the coming of Jesus Christ to this world, God fulfilled some of the promises He made to the Jews (Luke 1:72-73), and He will fulfill the rest of His promises as well. "For no matter how many promises God has made, they are 'Yes' in Christ" (2 Cor. 1:20, NIV).

Few passages in Scripture contain so much "distilled theology" as Micah 7:18-20. We see in them a reflection of what God told Moses on the mount (Ex. 34:5-7). The better we know the character of God, the more we can trust Him for the future. The better we know the promises and covenants of God, the more peace we will have in our hearts when things around us fall apart. When Micah wrote this confession of his faith, the future seemed hopeless; yet he had hope because he knew God and fully trusted Him.

No matter how dark the day, the light of God's promises is still shining. No matter how confusing and frightening our circumstances, the character of God remains the same.

You have every reason to trust Him!

Zephaniah in His Day

If the Hezekiah named in Zephaniah 1:1 is King Hezekiah (715–686), then the Prophet Zephaniah was his great-great-grandson. His name means "Jehovah hides" (i.e., "Jehovah protects") and describes God's ministry of protection for His faithful people when the day of His anger arrives (2:3).

Zephaniah's major theme is "the Day of the Lord," that period of time when God will judge the nations and usher in His righteous kingdom.[1] This theme is found in almost all the prophets, but it is particularly evident in Joel and Zephaniah. "The great Day of the Lord is near" (Zeph. 1:14, NIV).

The Scriptures reveal very little about Zephaniah's personal life. He ministered in Judah during the time of King Josiah (640–609), who led the nation in a religious reformation triggered by the finding of the Book of the Law in the temple in the year 622 (2 Chron. 34:14ff).[2] It's likely that Zephaniah preached prior to this reformation, or he would have said something about it in his book. Jeremiah and Zephaniah were contemporaries.

Politically, the times were in ferment. Assyria was losing its power, the Scythians were invading from the north, and Babylon had become the leading empire. King Manasseh (697–642) had led the people of Judah deeper and deeper into idolatry and the adoption of foreign ideas and customs, and Josiah had sought to reverse this trend. Alas, King Josiah died on the battlefield before his work was finished, and his successors on the throne allowed the people to return to their sinful ways.

A Suggested Outline of the Book of Zephaniah

Key theme: The coming Day of the Lord
Key verses: 1:14 and 2:3

I. The day of the Lord and the Jews—1:1–2:3
   1. Pictures of that great day
      (1) Like a flood—1:2-6
      (2) Like a great sacrifice—1:7-13
      (3) Like a battle—1:14-18
   2. Plea to the people: seek the Lord—2:1-3

II. The day of the Lord and the Gentiles—2:4-15
   1. Philistia—2:4-7
   2. Moab and Ammon—2:8-11
   3. Cush—2:12
   4. Assyria—2:13-15

III. The Day of the Lord and the kingdom—3:1-20
   1. Jerusalem: God's jealous anger—3:1-8
   2. The Gentiles: gracious forgiveness—3:9-10
   3. The remnant: bounteous blessing—3:11-20
      (1) The sinners removed—3:11-13
      (2) The believers rejoicing—3:14-17
      (3) The land restored—3:18-20

There's a Great Day Coming!

When was the last time you sang a hymn about the future judgment of the world? Most modern hymnals don't contain songs about "the Day of the Lord," and you certainly won't find the phrase in your daily newspaper or weekly news magazine. Even if they do believe in God, most people don't connect Him in any way with either current or future events. The closest we come to involving God in human events is when insurance policies mention "acts of God over which we have no control." But that's a far cry from Zephaniah's "the Day of the Lord."

Thinking people used to take God's judgment of the world seriously and even sang hymns about it. A famous medieval Latin hymn was based on Zephaniah 1:15, "That day is a day of wrath, a day of trouble and distress. . . ." The first two verses read:

> Day of wrath! O day of mourning!
> See fulfilled the prophet's warning,
> Heav'n and earth in ashes burning!

O what fear man's bosom rendeth
When from heav'n the Judge descendeth
On whose sentence all dependeth![3]

I wonder how popular a worship leader would be if he or she selected that particular hymn today?

"The Day of the Lord" is an important biblical concept that we must take seriously, because it tells us where things are going and how they're going to end. During "the Day of the Lord," God will send tribulation to the world, judge the nations, save His people Israel, and then establish His righteous kingdom. God warns the world that judgment is coming, and it's foolish for anybody to be unprepared. The big question is "Where will you hide on that great day?" (see Zeph. 2:3)

In the first two chapters of his book, the Prophet Zephaniah relates "the Day of the Lord" to both the Jews and the Gentiles.

1. The "Day of the Lord" and the Jews (Zeph. 1:1–2:4)

You would expect the great-great-grandson of King Hezekiah to be living comfortably in Jerusalem, enjoying a life of ease. Instead, you find him ministering as God's prophet, which was a dangerous calling. His contemporary Jeremiah was arrested and put in a filthy cistern for admonishing the leaders of Judah to surrender to the Babylonians.

God had shown Zephaniah that judgment was coming upon Judah in the form of the Babylonian Captivity, and the prophet had to share this message with the people. However, Babylon's invasion of Judah was but a feeble example of what would occur on that final "Day of the Lord," which would sweep over all the earth. Zephaniah opened his book by presenting *three graphic pictures of "the Day of the Lord."*

The first picture is that of *a devastating universal flood (Zeph. 1:2-3).* The Hebrew word translated "consume" in the

KJV means "to sweep away completely." The picture is that of total devastation of all that God created and is probably a reference to Noah's flood. (You find similar wording in Gen. 6:7; 7:4; 9:8-10.) God gave man dominion over the fish, the fowls, and the beasts (1:28; Ps. 8:7-8), but man lost that dominion when Adam disobeyed God. However, through Jesus Christ, man's lost dominion will one day be restored (Heb. 2:5-9).

God will not only destroy His creation, but He will also destroy the idols that people worship—the "stumbling blocks" that offend the Lord (Ezek. 14:1-8). In Zephaniah's day, idolatry was rife in Judah, thanks to the evil influence of King Manasseh. When God stretches out His hand, it means that judgment is coming (Isa. 9:12, 17, 21). The prophet names two of the false gods that had captured the hearts of the people: Baal, the rain god of the Canaanites (Zeph. 1:4), and Malcom (Milcom, Molech), the terrible god of the Ammonites (1 Kings 11:33; Amos 5:26). The people also worshiped the host of heaven (Deut. 4:19; Jer. 19:13; 32:29) and followed the godless example of the idolatrous priests ("Chemarim"[4] in Zeph. 1:4; see 2 Kings 23:5, 8; Hosea 10:5).

These idolaters may have claimed that they were still faithfully worshiping Jehovah, the true and living God, but Jehovah will not share worship or glory with any other god. In turning to idols, the people had turned away from the Lord and were not seeking Him or His blessing (Zeph. 1:6). They were guilty of sins of commission (worshiping idols) and omission (ignoring the Lord).

During the Babylonian Captivity, the Jews were cured of their fascination with foreign gods. Their temple was destroyed, their priesthood was scattered, and for seventy years they could not worship the way Moses had commanded them. When they were finally allowed to return to their land, one of the first things the Jews did was rebuild their temple and restore the sacrifices.

The second picture is that of *a great sacrifice (vv. 7-13)*. Since the Jewish people were accustomed to attending communal sacrifices (1 Sam. 9:11ff), this image was familiar to them. But this sacrifice would be different, for it was God who was hosting the sacrifice; His guests were the Babylonians; and the sacrifices to be offered were the people of Judah! No wonder the prophet called for silence as he contemplated such an awesome event![5] (See Amos 6:10; 8:3; Hab. 2:20.)

You would expect the royal family and the religious leaders[6] of the land to be the honored guests at God's feast, but they are the ones to be sacrificed! (Zeph. 1:8-9) God punishes them because they have abandoned His Word and adopted foreign practices, including wearing foreign clothes and worshiping foreign gods (see Num. 15:38; Deut. 22:11-12). After the death of King Josiah in 609, the last four kings of Judah were weak men, who yielded to the policies of the pro-Egyptian bloc in the government. Instead of trusting the Lord, they trusted their allies, and this led to disaster.

Zephaniah must have been a resident in Jerusalem, for he knew the layout of the city (Zeph. 1:10-13). When the Babylonians, God's guests, would come to the sacrificial feast, they would enter the city, plunder it, and then destroy it. The Fish Gate was where the fishermen had their markets; the "second quarter" was where the rich people lived in their fashionable houses, built from the wages owed to poor laborers. "Maktesh" was the market and business district of the city where the merchants and bankers were located.[7]

But the city would be destroyed, and the merchants' wealth confiscated. So thoroughly would the Babylonians do their work that they would search the city carefully and find even the people who were hiding.

The tragedy is that the invasion could have been avoided if the people had not been so complacent and indifferent toward what God was saying through His prophets. Judah was certain that the Lord was on their side because they were God's covenant people. They were like wine that sits undisturbed for a long time (Jer. 48:11; Amos 6:1) and congeals because it isn't poured from vessel to vessel to get rid of the bitter dregs. The worship of false gods had polluted the nation and the pure wine had become bitter.

The prophet's third picture of the "Day of the Lord" is that of *a great battle (Zeph. 1:14-18)*. The description is a vivid one: You can hear the cries of the captives and the shouts of the warriors; you can see thunderclouds of judgment and flashes of lightning; you behold the victims' blood poured out like cheap dust and their "entrails like filth" (v. 17, NIV). What a scene of destruction and carnage, and all because the nation refused to submit to the Word of the Lord. The fire of God's jealous zeal[8] would consume everything, and no one would escape. Even the wealthy would not be able to ransom their lives, and the enemy would take away their ill-gotten riches.

What Zephaniah describes here is but an illustration of what will happen in the end times when God's judgment falls on a wicked world, only that final "Day of the Lord" will be far more terrible (see Rev. 6–19). There will be cosmic disturbances that will affect the course of nature and cause people to cry out for a place to hide (Amos 5:18; 8:9; Joel 2:1-2, 10, 30-32; Rev. 6:12-17). Unless you know Jesus Christ as your own Savior, you will have no place to hide (Zeph. 2:3).

This explains why the prophet closed this message with a plea for the people to repent of their sins and turn to the Lord for His forgiveness (vv. 1-3). Like the Prophet Joel (2:16), he told them to call a solemn assembly and seek the Lord. Zephaniah especially called upon the godly remnant ("you meek of the earth") to pray and seek God's face, perhaps referring to the promise in 2 Chronicles 7:14. But even if the majority of the nation followed false gods and turned away from the Lord, God would still protect His own precious remnant when the Day of Judgment comes (Mal. 3:16-18).

Zephaniah and Jeremiah ministered during the same period in history, and both of them begged the rulers to trust God and turn from sin, but the kings, officials, and priests refused to obey. God would have rescued the nation at the last minute, but the leaders were insensitive to God's call and disobedient to His Word.

But the Lord did spare a godly remnant that stayed true to Him throughout the seventy years of captivity. They were a "company of the concerned," who became the nucleus of the restored nation when they returned to the land. In every period in history it is the godly remnant that keeps the light burning when it seems like the darkness is about to cover the earth. Today, God needs a "company of the concerned," who will walk the narrow road regardless of what others may do, obey God's Word, and share His Gospel with the lost. God is keeping His "book of remembrance" (Mal. 3:16-17), and you and I want our names in that book.

2. The "Day of the Lord" and the Gentiles (Zeph. 2:4-15)

God's judgment begins in the house of the Lord (1 Peter 4:17), which explains why Zephaniah started with the people of Judah; but now he explains how "the Day of the Lord" will affect the Gentile nations surrounding Judah. Though they were never given God's Law as were the Jews (Ps. 147:19-20), the Gentiles are still responsible before God; for God has revealed Himself to them in creation and conscience (Rom. 1:18ff). Furthermore, these nations had not always treated the Jews kindly, and now the time had arrived for God to judge them.

The nations named may represent all the Gentiles, since these nations correspond to the four points of the compass: Assyria (north), Cush (south), Moab and Ammon (east) and Philistia (west). During the great "Day of the Lord," all the nations of the earth will taste the judgment of God.

Philistia (Zeph. 2:4-7). The Philistines were ancient enemies of the Jews (Gen. 20–21, 26). According to Amos 1:6-8, they took Jewish people captive from cities in southern Judah and sold them to other nations as slaves. But the time would come when their populous cities would be empty and their land left desolate, a place for shepherds to feed their flocks. Their coastal cities, made wealthy by vast shipping enterprises, would be destroyed by the enemy and left in ruins. Nebuchadnezzar invaded Philistia and conquered it, and the only remnant of that great nation left today is the name "Palestine," which comes from "Philistine" (see Ezek. 25:15–28:26).

However, the Jews will inhabit the land of the Philistines when the kingdom is established, and the Lord will enable them to live in peace. Zephaniah will later have more to say about this when he describes the kingdom blessings (Zeph. 3:9-20).

Moab and Ammon (Zeph. 2:8-11). The Moabites and Ammonites originated from Lot's incestuous union with his two daughters (Gen. 19:30-38) and were hateful enemies of the Jews (Num. 22; Jud. 3; 10; 1 Sam. 11:1-5; 2 Sam. 12:26ff). But these two arrogant nations would end up like Sodom and Gomorrah, wiped off the face of the earth (Gen. 19; note the connection here with Lot). No more would they insult either the nation of Israel or the God of Israel. (See Amos 1:13–2:3 for further evidence of the wickedness and inhumanity of these two nations.) Once again, the prophet promised that the Jews would occupy the land of their enemies when the kingdom is established (see also Ezek. 25:1-11).

Cush (Zeph. 2:12). This nation was located in the upper Nile region. Some students think the reference includes Egypt, another long-time enemy of the Jews. It was Nebuchadnezzar and the swords of the Babylonian soldiers that conquered this ancient nation (Ezek. 30:4-5).

Assyria (Zeph. 2:13-15). Until the rise of Babylon, Assyria had been the dominant power, a ruthless people who were notorious for their pride and their cruelty to their enemies. A century and a half before, God had sent the Prophet Jonah to Assyria's capital city of Nineveh to warn them of God's judgment, and the people had repented, but successive generations went back to the old pagan ways, and Nineveh was destroyed in 612. Within the next few years, the once great Assyrian Empire simply vanished from the face of the earth, and Zephaniah saw it coming.

Because Nineveh thought it was an impregnable city, her citizens were careless and carefree when Zephaniah made his prediction, but God brought both the people and their city down into the dust of defeat. (See the Book of Nahum and Isa. 45; 47:10.)

Since the predictions about the destruction of these nations have all come true, isn't it reasonable to assume that Zephaniah's other predictions will also be fulfilled? Each of these local invasions and conquests was a precursor of the end times "Day of the Lord," which will come upon the whole world. But when the "Day of the Lord" has run its course, Israel will be delivered, and the Lord will establish His glorious kingdom on the earth. In the last chapter of his prophecy, Zephaniah explains how the "Day of the Lord" will relate to this promised kingdom.

Before we leave Zephaniah 1 and 2, we must note some practical truths that apply to believers today. First, God judges His people when they deliberately disobey His Law. His people are to be different from the other nations and not imitate their ways or worship their gods (Num. 23:9; Ex. 33:16; Deut. 32:8). "Be not conformed to this world" is an admonition for all believers today (Rom. 12:2; see 2 Cor. 6:14–7:1).

Second, God's promise to Abraham still stands: Those

who bless Israel, God will bless; those who curse Israel, God will curse (Gen. 12:1-3). The nations that have sinned against God by mistreating the Jews can expect Him to judge them.

Finally, God's Word is true and will be fulfilled in its time. God's people can claim His promises and know that their God will be faithful, and God's enemies can be sure that His words of warning carry costly penalties. "It is a fearful thing to fall into the hands of the living God" (Heb. 10:31).

The Glory of the Kingdom

Why did the prophets consistently close their books with messages of hope? For at least three reasons. To begin with, hope is a great motivation for obedience, and the prophets wanted to encourage God's people to submit to God's will and do what He commanded. God's covenant blessings come to His people only when they obey His covenant conditions.

A second reason is the prophets' emphases on the faithfulness of God. The Lord will keep His promises and one day establish the kingdom; and since God is faithful to keep His promises, we ought to be faithful in obeying His Word. If we obey, God will be faithful to bless; if we disobey, He will be faithful to chasten; if we confess, He will be faithful to forgive.

Finally, the closing message of hope was an encouragement to the faithful remnant in the land, who were true to God and suffered because of their devotion to Him. It's difficult to belong to that "company of the committed" who stand true to the Lord and His Word no matter what others may do or say. Knowing that God would one day defeat their enemies and reign in righteousness would encourage the believing remnant to persist in their faithful walk with the Lord.

In this last chapter, God reveals His plans for Jerusalem, the Gentile nations, and the faithful remnant. At the same time, the Lord reveals Himself and His gracious working on behalf of His people in every age and in every place.

1. Jerusalem: God's jealous anger (Zeph. 3:1-8)

Jerusalem is commonly called "the holy city,"[1] but in Zephaniah's day, the city didn't manifest much holiness! Isaiah (1:21ff), Jeremiah (29:12ff), and Ezekiel (4–6, 9) gave the same assessment in their day. Even the Gentiles called Jerusalem "the rebellious and the wicked city" (Ezra 4:12, 15), and they could cite proof for their statement.

A sinning people (Zeph. 3:1-2). Instead of being holy, the city was filthy and polluted because of shameful sin; and instead of bringing peace ("Jerusalem" means "city of peace"), the city was guilty of rebellion and oppression. God gave His people the revelation of Himself in His Word and His mighty acts, yet they didn't believe Him or seek Him. "Draw near to God and He will draw near to you. Cleanse your hands, you sinners; and purify your hearts, you double-minded" (James 4:8, NKJV).

A godless leadership (Zeph. 3:3-4). God expected the civil and religious leaders of the land to take His Word seriously and lead the people in the way of righteousness. Instead, the leaders acted like ravenous beasts in the way they oppressed the people and took what they wanted from them. The prophets were unfaithful to the Lord and His Word and dealt treacherously with the people. They didn't proclaim God's truth; they only preached what the people wanted to hear.

As for the priests, their very ministry was toxic and polluted the sanctuary! (Matt. 23:25-28 relates what Jesus said about the Pharisees in His day.) Instead of serving God for His glory, the priests twisted the Law to please themselves and gain what they wanted.

The tragedy is that God had spoken to His people and corrected them in discipline, and yet they wouldn't listen or obey (Zeph. 3:2). "If in spite of these things you do not accept My correction but continue to be hostile toward Me, I Myself will be hostile toward you and will afflict you for your sins seven times over" (Lev. 26:23-24, NIV). This was the message of Jeremiah to the city of Jerusalem even while Babylon was poised to attack (Jer. 2:30; 5:3; 7:28; 17:23; 32:33).

A righteous God (Zeph. 3:5-8). God's name was identified with the city and the temple (2 Sam. 7:13; 1 Kings 5:5; Neh. 1:9), and yet both were cesspools of iniquity. Therefore, He would have to act in judgment for His own name's sake. The wicked officials met at the city gate morning after morning to transact their evil business, and the Lord was there to behold their deeds. How patiently He waited, and yet they would not repent and turn to Him for cleansing!

Since the Lord reminded His people that He had judged the Gentiles and cut off nations (Zeph. 3:6), He was able to cut Judah off as well. In fact, the Jews were more guilty than were the Gentiles because the Lord had given Israel more truth and more blessing. The people were sinning against a flood of light. Surely God's judgment of the other nations should have awakened the Jews to their peril, but they paid no attention. After all, they were God's covenant people, and He would protect them from their enemies. They forgot that covenant privileges also involved covenant responsibilities.

The Lord concludes this message to Jerusalem by describing a courtroom scene in which He stands to testify against His people (v. 8). While the impending Babylonian Captivity is involved here, there is also an end-times application in the Battle of Armageddon, when the nations of the world converge against Jerusalem. God will pour out His wrath upon these nations, deliver His people, and establish His kingdom (Zech. 14:1-9). His jealous anger will burn like fire against all who resist His truth and disobey His Word. The terrible "Day of the Lord" will dawn and there will be no escape (see Zeph. 1:2ff).

2. The Gentiles: God's gracious forgiveness (Zeph. 3:9-10)

It's important to keep in mind that God's call of Abraham involved bringing God's blessing to the whole world (Gen. 12:1-3). God accomplished this by giving the Jews the knowledge of the true God, the written Word of God, and the Savior, Jesus Christ (Rom. 9:1-5). Therefore, they were to share these blessings with the Gentiles.

The Jews were supposed to magnify the Lord's name before the Gentiles. Instead, they imitated the pagan nations and disgraced God's name (Isa. 52:5; Rom. 2:24). The court of the Gentiles in the Jewish temple was supposed to be the place where Gentiles could talk with Jews about the true God and even pray to Him, but the religious leaders made that area into a market for selling sacrifices and exchanging money. What kind of testimony was that to the outsiders who were earnestly seeking truth?

What blessings does God promise for the Gentiles in the last days? First, He promises that *the Gentiles shall be converted (Zeph. 3:9).* Instead of calling on their false gods, the Gentiles will call upon the true and living God and have their lips purified. Since what we say with our lips comes from the heart (Matt. 12:34-35), cleansed lips indicate forgiven sin and a cleansed heart (Isa. 6:1-8).

But the Gentiles will do much more than call on the Lord and receive His cleansing; they will also *serve the Lord as one people* and no longer be divided ("serve Him shoulder to shoulder," Zeph. 3:9, NIV). The prophets teach that during the Kingdom Age the Gentiles will go to Jerusalem to worship and serve the Lord (Isa. 2:1-5; 4:1-6; Ezek. 40–48; Zech.

14:9ff).[2] The God of Israel will be the Lord of all the earth, and the Gentile nations will honor and serve Him. Along with the scattered Israelites who return to their land, the Gentiles will bring the Lord offerings and be called His "worshipers."

Before our Lord's death on the cross, there was a vast difference between the relationship of Jews and Gentiles to each other and to the Lord. But the middle wall that separated them has now been taken down (Eph. 2:11ff), and both can share in the spiritual blessings that come through faith in Christ. "For there is no difference between the Jew and the Greek: for the same Lord over all is rich unto all that call upon Him. For whosoever shall call upon the name of the Lord shall be saved" (Rom. 10:12-13). This miracle of God's grace will be demonstrated in the Kingdom Age as the Gentile nations trust and worship the God of Israel.

3. The remnant: God's bounteous blessing (Zeph. 3:11-20)

When the terrible "Day of the Lord" is over, Israel will be a new nation. The Jews will look by faith upon the Messiah whom they crucified, believe in Him, and enter into a new life in the promised kingdom.

Sin will be removed (Zeph. 3:11-13). The Jews won't have to be "put to shame" because, when they see Christ, they will be ashamed of what they did to the Lord and will mourn over their transgressions (Zech. 12:10–13:1). It will be a time of deep repentance and confession that will lead to salvation. God will especially deal with the pride of Israel that for centuries had kept them from submitting humbly to the righteousness of God that comes only by faith in Christ (Rom. 9:30–10:13; Phil. 3:1-12). There will be no place on God's holy hill for proud sinners who think they can earn God's salvation by their good works. In contrast to the proud sinners will be the believing remnant, the "meek and humble, who trust in the name of the Lord" (Zeph. 3:12, NIV).

Faith in Christ will make everything new so that the people will no longer disobey God or practice deception. This suggests that all love of idolatry will be taken from their hearts, for idols are lies and to worship them is to practice deception. For the first time in centuries, the Jews will be able to enjoy their meals and their sleep, for all their enemies will have been defeated. During the years of their worldwide dispersion, in many places the Jews have been subjected to threats and intimidation, even fearing for their lives (Deut. 28:63-68), but that will end when God establishes the kingdom and Christ reigns over the nations.

God's people will rejoice (Zeph. 3:14-17). This is one of the most poignant passages in Scripture. It depicts the Lord as a loving mother, singing over her children and finding joy in their presence. The people of God sing and shout because of all that God has done for them. He has taken away their punishment, defeated their enemies, and come to dwell with them. Furthermore, He has guaranteed that the people of Israel will never again be afraid. Because the Lord is the King of Israel, His people have nothing to fear.

When Pilate presented a suffering Jesus to the Jewish leaders, they rejected Him and shouted, "We have no king but Caesar" (John 19:15). But now the Jewish people will joyfully acknowledge that Jesus Christ is King of Kings and Lord of Lords (Phil. 2:9-11). Instead of standing dejectedly like defeated prisoners of war, the Jews will enthusiastically shout God's praises.

What do they have to sing about? To begin with, they have God's presence with them and God's power working for them (Zeph. 3:17). Even more, their God holds them next to His heart like a loving mother holds a baby; He quiets them with His love,[3] and He even sings to them! This image of "the motherhood of God" assures forgiven sinners that God is with them, that He loves them, and that they have nothing to fear.[4]

Our God is a "singing" God. God the Father sings to the Jewish remnant entering the kingdom (v. 17). God the Son sang at the close of the Passover Feast, and then went to the garden to pray (Matt. 26:30). He also sang after His triumphant resurrection from the dead (Ps. 22:22; Heb. 2:12). God the Spirit sings today through the hearts and lips of Christians who praise God in the Spirit (Eph. 5:18-21).

The nation will be restored (Zeph. 3:18-20). During the seventy years of captivity in Babylon, and then during their worldwide dispersion among the Gentiles after A.D. 70, devout Jews were not able to celebrate their appointed feasts (Lev. 23). Since the destruction of the temple in A.D. 70, the Jewish people have had no temple, altar, priesthood, or sacrifice (Hosea 3:4-5). Of course, the types and symbols of the Old Testament Law have all been fulfilled in Christ, including the feasts and sacrifices (Heb. 10), but Zephaniah intimates that these feasts will be restored in the Kingdom Age, and Zechariah 14:16-21 seems to support this interpretation.

Why would the Lord restore religious practices that have now been fulfilled? Possibly as a means of teaching Israel the meaning of the doctrine of salvation through Jesus Christ. The feasts described in Leviticus 23 picture "salvation history," from the slaying of the Passover lamb (John 1:29) to the Day of Atonement (the cleansing of Israel) and the Feast of Tabernacles (the Kingdom Age). The Prophet Ezekiel describes in great detail the structure and services of a great temple in Israel (Ezek. 40–48), and this includes the offering of the levitical sacrifices. Just as the Old Testament types looked forward to the coming of the Savior, perhaps during the Kingdom Age these rituals will look back to His finished work.

God's promise is that His scattered people will be gathered, His lame people will be rescued, and His sinful people will be forgiven and no longer bear the shame of their wicked deeds. "I will bring you home" (Zeph. 3:20, NIV) is God's gracious promise, and He will keep it. Where once the Jewish nation brought shame and disgrace to God's name and were poor witnesses to the Gentiles, now Israel will bring honor and praise to the Lord their God and reveal to the Gentile nations the glory of His name. Israel will receive honor from the Gentiles and give the glory to the Lord.

The State of Israel was "born" on May 14, 1948, but that event, significant as it is, was not the fulfillment of God's promise to regather His people and restore their fortunes. That promise will be fulfilled in the end times, after the Jews have experienced the "Day of the Lord" and been prepared to see their Messiah. But God's promises will be fulfilled, and God's people Israel will be restored and bring worldwide glory to the God of Abraham, Isaac, and Jacob, the God and Father of our Lord Jesus Christ.

But there is a present-day practical lesson here for any of God's people who have strayed from His will and have experienced His chastening. When you come to Him with a broken heart, confessing your sins, He will receive you the way a loving mother receives a disobedient child. He will love you and even sing to you! He will bring peace to your heart and "quiet you in His love." Yes, we suffer for our disobedience; and sometimes we carry the scars of that disobedience for the rest of our lives. But the Lord will forgive us (1 John 1:9), forget our sins, and restore us into His loving fellowship.

Dr. William Culbertson, late president of Moody Bible Institute, sometimes ended his public prayers with, "And Lord, help us bear the consequences of forgiven sin and to end well." There are consequences to *forgiven* sin; for though God in His grace cleanses us, God in His government says, "You will reap what you have sown." After King David confessed his sin, the Prophet Nathan assured him that the Lord had put away his sin, but for the rest of his days, David suffered the tragic consequences of what he had done (2 Sam. 12:1-15).

But when God establishes His kingdom on earth, He will restore His people, renew the land, and give His people a new beginning that will cause them to forget their past disobedience and focus on praising the Lord and glorifying His name.

Jehovah is "the God of hope." Therefore, He can fill us with "all joy and peace in believing" so that we can "abound in hope by the power of the Holy Spirit" (Rom. 15:13, NKJV).

Is that your experience today?

You in Your Time

It does us little good to learn about the times of the Minor Prophets if we don't do something about our own times.

Situations vary from nation to nation, but the statistics for my own country aren't too encouraging.[1]

- Since 1960, the rate of births to unmarried teenagers has increased almost 200 percent.
- Since 1960, violent crime has increased by 560 percent.
- The fastest growing segment of the criminal population is children. Between 1982 and 1991, the arrest rate for juvenile murder increased 93 percent.
- The average child will watch up to 8,000 murders and 100,000 acts of violence on TV by the time he or she leaves grade school.
- Eight out of ten Americans can expect to be the victim of violent crime at least once in their lives.
- Since 1960, teen suicides have more than tripled. It is now the second leading cause of death among teens.
- The top problems in high schools are alcohol and drug abuse, pregnancy, suicide, rape, and robbery.

As go the homes, churches, and schools, so goes the nation. It's time to be concerned.

T H I R T E E N

The Company of the Concerned

One of the key truths found in the Minor Prophets is the presence of a godly remnant in times of moral and spiritual decay. This remnant is a small group of people whose devotion to the Lord can make a difference in the nation. After all, if God had found as many as ten righteous people in Sodom, He would have spared the whole city! (Gen. 18:32)

Israel was at its lowest ebb during the Period of the Judges. Yet God could always find a dedicated man or woman to lead His armies to deliver His people. Elijah thought he was the only faithful person left in the land, but God informed him that He had 7,000 who hadn't bowed the knee to Baal (1 Kings 19:18). The Prophet Isaiah wrote, "Unless the Lord of hosts had left to us a very small remnant, we would have become like Sodom, we would have been made like Gomorrah" (Isa. 1:9, NKJV).

I like to call this godly remnant "the company of the concerned." They are people who are truly concerned about the will of the Lord and the character of their country, people who are distressed by evil and want to do something about it. The Prophet Ezekiel had a vision of the remnant in his day: "Go through the midst of the city, through the midst of Jerusalem, and set a mark upon the foreheads of the men that sigh and that cry for all the abominations that be done in the midst thereof" (Ezek. 9:4). The NIV translates "sigh" and "cry" as "grieve" and "lament."

Whoever wrote Psalm 119 belonged to the "sighers and criers" of his day. "Indignation grips me," he wrote, "because of the wicked, who have forsaken Your Law" (v. 53, NIV); and he confessed, "I am a companion of all those who fear You, and of those who keep Your precepts" (v. 63, NKJV). He was an encouragement to others who belonged to the "company of the concerned," for he said, "Those who fear You will be glad when they see me, because I have hoped in Your word" (v. 74, NKJV). And he told the careless sinners in the land, "Depart from me, you evildoers, for I will keep the commandments of my God!" (v. 115, NKJV)

But I need to make one thing clear from the beginning: I'm not talking about people motivated by *anger* so much as by *anguish*. Certainly there's a place for righteous anger in the Christian life (Eph. 4:26), but anger alone may do more harm than good. "For the wrath of man does not produce the righteousness of God" (James 1:20, NKJV). When righteous anger is mingled with compassion, you have anguish; and anguish is what the "company of the concerned" feel as they behold the moral and spiritual decline of the nation. "Rivers of water run down from my eyes, because men do not keep Your Law" (Ps. 119:136, NKJV). "Trouble and anguish have overtaken me, yet Your commandments are my delights" (v. 143, NKJV).

Each of the prophets whose writings we have studied belonged to the "company of the concerned," and they are good examples for us to follow.

First, *they were totally committed to the Lord.* Amos was an ordinary farmer and shepherd, untrained in the schools of the prophets; yet God called him to deliver His message at a strategic time in history. As I travel in ministry, I'm more and more impressed by the "lay people" God has called to serve Him in significant places, people who have no professional "ministerial training," yet who are doing great things for the glory of the Lord.[2] Robert Murray M'Cheyne wrote, "It is not great talents God blesses so much as great likeness to Jesus. A holy minister is an awful weapon in the hand of God."

The "company of the concerned" is made up of people who are separated from sin (Rom. 12:1-2; 2 Cor. 6:14–7:1), but who are not isolated from the real world. They aren't "holier than thou" in their attitude toward sinners. They have the courage to be different (but not odd) and to walk the narrow road no matter what it may cost them. They are people who pray consistently for those in authority (1 Tim. 2:1-4). It does no good to write letters and protest if we aren't praying for those leading our nation.

Second, the "company of the committed" is composed of people who have *a proper fear of God in their hearts*. The prophets certainly teach the love of God toward His people and toward lost sinners, but they also remind us that "our God is a consuming fire" (Heb. 12:29). They believed the Word of God and knew that judgment was coming to the land.

The only nation on earth that is in a special covenant relationship with God is the nation of Israel. While many of the founding fathers of the United States of America were God-fearing men, the people of the United States can't claim special privileges from God because of their citizenship. It's true that the Puritan forefathers felt called to build God's kingdom on American soil, but we have no biblical basis for their vision.

What do we have? The promises of God for those of His people who will obey 2 Chronicles 7:14 and intercede for their country. God works in response to believing prayer, and believing prayer must be based on the Word of God.

The fear of the Lord is the fear that conquers every fear.

John Wesley said, "Give me one hundred preachers who fear nothing but sin and desire nothing but God, and I care not a straw whether they be clergymen or laymen, such alone will shake the gates of hell and set up the kingdom of God on earth." He was describing the "company of the concerned."

Third, the company of the concerned" is indeed a *company,* composed of believers who realize that God wants His people to "flock together" and not try to do everything alone. The most dangerous believers are those who aren't accountable to anybody but do whatever they please and think they're serving God. They write angry letters to government officials, media people, and even local pastors, and often they don't sign their names. God has called them to set everything right in the world, even though they often don't really understand the problems they're trying to solve. Instead of belonging to the "company of the concerned," they're charter members of The Company of the Confused.

Malachi 3:16 is a good description of the kind of "company" God is looking for: "Then those who feared the Lord spoke to one another, and the Lord listened and heard them; so a book of remembrance was written before Him for those who fear the Lord and who meditate in His name" (NKJV). "The more the truths by which we believe are contradicted," said Alexander Maclaren, "the more should we commune with fellow-believers." When you study the "one another" statements of the New Testament, you discover how much Christians need one another and need to minister to one another. It has well been said that you can't raise one Christian any more than you can raise one bee.

To be sure, every local church has its weaknesses and faults, but it's the family of God, and that's where we belong. Nobody was born into a perfect family. Yet we love our brothers and sisters and try to ignore the things that irritate us. When Jesus sent out the twelve apostles, He sent them out two-by-two, because "two are better than one" (Ecc. 4:9). People who are a part of the "company of the concerned" don't try to go it alone. They love one another, pray for one another, and seek to encourage one another.

Something else is true: They realize the importance of righteousness and justice in the land. "Righteousness exalts a nation, but sin is a reproach to any people" (Prov. 14:34, NKJV). The believers in the "company of the concerned" seek to be salt and light in the land (Matt. 5:13-16) and do all they can to prevent decay and dispel darkness. The influence of their character, conduct, and witness promotes righteousness, whether it's in their daily work, the way they vote or pay their taxes, their example, the way they raise their children, or how they invest their time and money.

Nehemiah is a person who exemplifies what it means to be in the "company of the concerned." When he heard about the tragic condition of Jerusalem, he sat down and wept, knelt down and prayed, and then stood up and worked to change things (Neh. 1–2). He could have excused himself by arguing, "It's not my fault that Jerusalem is in ruins," or "I have a job to do right here in the palace." Nehemiah never read the words of Edmund Burke, but he lived by them: "It is necessary only for the good man to do nothing for evil to triumph."

When you read the Book of Nehemiah, you meet a man who enlisted the help of the Jewish leaders and rallied the common people to rebuild the wall of the city. He didn't try to do it alone. He was a man of prayer who trusted God to supply the needs and defeat the enemies around Jerusalem. In fifty-two days, the job was done, and the song of praise from Jerusalem could be heard for miles.

Much more can be said about the "company of the concerned," but let me close with this observation: These people know the importance of good leadership in the nation. "Everything rises and falls with leadership," claims Dr. Lee

Roberson, and he's right. However, during the times of the prophets, the leaders of Israel and Judah were too often selfish, disobedient to God's Law, and unwilling to trust Him for the wisdom and help that they needed. The prophets warned the kings, princes, and priests that their sins would ruin the nation, but the men refused to listen. After Judah was ravaged and Jerusalem and the temple ruined, Jeremiah wrote that it had been caused by "the sins of her prophets, and the iniquities of her priests" (Lam. 4:13).

A democracy is not a theocracy, where the king is God's representative on earth; nor is a pluralistic society the same as the homogeneous society of the Jewish people, who were all governed by the same moral code. But leaders in a democracy should still be expected to be men and women of character, who practice honesty and integrity and who genuinely care for their people. Someone has said that a politician is concerned about his party and asks, "Is it popular?" The diplomat is concerned about policy and asks, "Is it safe?" But the statesman is concerned about the good of the nation and asks, "Is it right?"

Edward Everett Hale, author of *The Man without a Country*, wrote:

> I am only one, but still I am one. I cannot do everything, but still I can do something. And because I cannot do everything, I will not refuse to do the something that I can do.

That's a good motto for the "company of the concerned." But add to it the great words of Paul: "I can do all things through Christ who strengthens me . . . for it is God who works in you both to will and to do for His good pleasure" (Phil. 4:13; 2:13, NKJV).

It's time to be concerned.

Personal and Group Study Guide

For Personal Study

Settle into your favorite chair with your Bible, a pen or pencil, and this book. Read a chapter, marking portions that seem significant to you. Write in the margins. Note where you agree, disagree, or question the author. Look at the endnotes and relevant Scripture passages. Then turn to the questions listed in this study guide. If you want to trace your progress with a written record, use a notebook to record your answers, thoughts, feelings, and further questions. Refer to the text and to the Scriptures as you allow the questions to enlarge your thinking. And *pray*. Ask God to give you a discerning mind for truth, an active concern for others, and a greater love for Himself.

For Group Study

Plan ahead. Before meeting with your group, read and mark the chapter as if you were preparing for personal study. Glance through the questions making mental notes of how you might contribute to your group's discussion. Bring a Bible and the text to your meeting.

Arrange an environment that promotes discussion. Comfortable chairs arranged in a casual circle invite people to talk with each other. Then say, "We are here to listen and respond to each other—and to learn together." If you are the leader, simply be sure to sit where you can have eye contact with each person.

Promptness counts. Time is as valuable to many people as money. If the group runs late (because of a late start), these people will feel as robbed as if you had picked their pockets. So, unless you have a mutual agreement, begin and end on time.

Involve everyone. Group learning works best if everyone participates more or less equally. If you are a natural *talker*, pause before you enter the conversation. Then ask a quiet person what he or she thinks. If you are a natural *listener*, don't hesitate to jump into the discussion. Others will benefit from your thoughts—but only if you speak them. If you are the *leader*, be careful not to dominate the session. Of course, you will have thought about the study ahead of time, but don't assume that people are present just to hear you—as flattering as that may feel. Instead, help group members to make their own discoveries. Ask the questions, but insert your own ideas only as they are needed to fill gaps.

Pace the study. The questions for each session are designed to last about one hour. Early questions form the framework for later discussion, so don't rush by so quickly that you miss a valuable foundation. Later questions, however, often speak of the here and now. So don't dawdle so long at the beginning that you leave no time to "get personal." While the leader must take responsibility for timing the flow of questions, it is the job of each person in the group to assist in keeping the study moving at an even pace.

Pray for each other—together, or alone. Then watch God's hand at work in all of your lives.

Notice that each session includes the following features:

Session Topic—a brief statement summarizing the session.

Community Builder—an activity to get acquainted with the session topic and/or with each other.

Group Discussion Questions—a list of questions to encourage individual or group discovery and application.

Optional Activities—supplemental ideas that will enhance the study.

Prayer Focus—suggestions for turning one's learning into prayer.

Assignment—activities or preparation to complete prior to the next session.

Chapter One
The Lion Roars!
(Amos 1:1–2:16)

Session Topic
When God's patience had run out, Amos was sent to announce that God's judgment against sin was soon coming to six Gentile nations and also to Judah and Israel.

Community Builders
1. How would you describe the books of the Minor Prophets to someone not familiar with the Bible? Write your answer on a piece of paper and save it for comparison at the end of the study.

2. As you have seen, the title of this study is *Be Concerned.* Brainstorm together as a group what concerns you about your church and nation.

Group Discussion Questions
1. What might have been the expected response of the six Gentile nations to whom Amos spoke? Why did God send these messages to them?

2. The Edomites "cast off all pity" (KJV) or "stifled His compassion" (NASB) toward the Jews. How is this possible? What was the result? See also Romans 1:18, "suppress the truth in unrighteousness."

3. If it was so sinful for the Ammonites to kill women and unborn children (Amos 1:13), how can we understand God's commands to the Israelites to do the same to their enemies? (See Josh 6:20-21; 11:8, 11, 14-15; Deut. 9:4; Jud. 2:1-3.)

4. Wiersbe observes that the Jews were probably glad to hear of the judgment coming to the Gentile nations. When have you felt glad about someone else's punishment? In what situations, if ever, is it justified to feel this way? (Cf. Rom.

12:17-21 with Rev. 6:9-10.)

5. What was the condition of Judah and Israel during the time of Amos?

6. Why was Judah to be judged? How was their judgment different from that of the Gentile nations?

7. What were Israel's three flagrant sins? What do you think are the most flagrant sins of the church today?

8. What did Amos convey about the future of Israel?

9. Wiersbe states that these prophets proclaimed "the goodness and severity of God" (Rom. 11:22). We are well-acquainted with God's goodness; in what manner do you see God displaying His "severity" today?

10. In Matthew 23 (especially v. 28) Jesus accuses the scribes and Pharisees of the same sins as Judah in the days of Amos. What temptations do you face in striving against this type of sin?

Optional Activities

1. The Israelites were enjoying peace and prosperity, and yet God was not pleased with them. If peace and prosperity do not necessarily signify God's approval, how can we know when God is pleased with us? Search the Scriptures for your answer.

2. Wiersbe explains that "the Law of Moses clearly governed how the slaves were treated." If you were a Christian living in the Civil War era, how would you biblically explain God's view of slavery?

Prayer Focus

Praise God for His absolute holiness, and for giving His Son to be punished for our sin in our place. Ask God to help you listen to His voice and act upon it.

Assignment

1. Read Amos 3:1-15.

2. Read chapter 2 of *Be Concerned*, and look over the study guide.

Chapter Two

Listen to What God Says
(Amos 3:1-15)

Session Topic
Amos delivered three messages from the Lord to the nation of Israel: an explanation of the divine calls, an accusation of their sin, and a lamentation of the nation's coming doom.

Community Builders
1. What is the most inspiring story you've heard about someone who, even though unlikely, was used by God in a powerful way?

2. How do you decide where to draw the line between what is unnecessary affluence and what is needed to live in our culture? In what ways have your views on this changed over time?

Group Discussion Questions
1. How can we make sure we are really listening to God and not hardening our hearts?

2. What were four characteristics of God's divine calling of Israel? Briefly explain each one.

3. Why did the Lord single out the Jewish nation to be His special people? (See Gen 12:2-3; Deut. 7:6-8a, 9:6; Isa. 49:6; Gal. 3:8; Rom. 11:28-36.)

4. As believers, chosen people of God, how are we to live?

5. Why did God call a prophet at this time? Why did He call Amos?

6. Who else in the Bible was unexpectedly called of God for a powerful ministry?

7. How do education, natural talent, or personality fit into God's call?

8. What was Israel being punished for? (Amos 3:10)

9. How can you and/or your church show more care for widows, orphans, the poor, and strangers?

10. In what way are you "addicted to affluence"? What influences are feeding this addiction? What guidance does the Bible give regarding temptation? (See Matt. 4:1-11; 1 Cor. 10:12-14; Heb. 4:15-16.)

Optional Activities

1. Examine your heart regarding your own feelings of adequacy to do the work of the Lord. Offer yourself to the Lord again as a willing vessel.

2. Meditate on and memorize 2 Corinthians 3:4-6.

Prayer Focus

Thank God that He speaks to people through the prophets, His Son, and through His Word. Ask God for ears to hear and a heart to obey.

Assignment

1. Read Amos 4:1-13.

2. Read chapter 3 of *Be Concerned*, and look over the study guide.

Chapter Three

Sins in Good Standing
(Amos 4:1-13)

Session Topic
Living in luxury, being hypocritical in their religion, and being obstinate toward God's warnings were all sins which were grieving the Lord and ruining the kingdom of Israel.

Community Builders
1. Read aloud James 5:1-5. Who is this passage meant for? What is its message for you?

2. At what times do you find yourself with "aimless leisure"? How does the Sabbath fit into this?

Group Discussion Questions
1. Of the three particular sins that Amos addressed against Israel, which do you believe is the biggest problem in the churches of our culture today? Why?

2. Parents usually want "the best" for their children. What is "the best"?

3. What religious activity have you done in a "playacting" manner?

4. When, if ever, would there be a place for going to church when you don't feel like it?

5. According to Wiersbe, what is the test of a true spiritual experience?

6. If a Christian were having a hard time cheerfully giving or sacrificing to the Lord, what should that person do?

7. Wiersbe states, "Any religious 'revival' that doesn't alter the priorities of Christians and help solve the problems in society is not a 'revival' at all." In all the calls for revival that we hear today, where does alleviating societal problems fit in?

8. What did God send to Israel to bring His people back to Himself? How has God brought you back to Himself?

9. It became too late for Israel to repent. When, if ever, would it be too late for a person living now to repent? (See Heb. 6:4-6; Luke 23:39-43.)

Optional Activities
1. At your next gathering of believers, ask yourself the questions Wiersbe suggests such as: "Is God getting the glory?" "Is there a brokenness before Him?" "Does the fruit remain?" Consider what you can contribute to a Christ-centered gathering.

2. Memorize and meditate on 1 Timothy 6:17-19.

Prayer Focus
Thank God for the moving of the Spirit, for true spiritual experiences, and for revival. Ask God to help you be prepared for the day of His coming.

Assignment
1. Read Amos 5:1-17.

2. Read chapter 4 of *Be Concerned*, and look over the study guide.

Chapter Four

How to Avoid the Storm
(Amos 5:1-17)

Session Topic
Even as Amos lamented Israel's coming destruction, he pleaded with the Israelites to return to the Lord.

Community Builders
1. What does seeking the Lord mean to you? Share times when you realized you were seeking the experience rather than the Lord. What role does "the experience" have in our movement toward the Lord?

2. Discuss Wiersbe's list of three motivations to seek the Lord. What motivates you to seek the Lord?

Group Discussion Questions
1. What did Amos plead with the people of Israel for?

2. What do you think of Wiersbe's statement, "The way we treat God's Word is the way we treat God, and the way we treat God's messengers is the way we treat the Lord Himself"?

3. What do nations usually depend on? How would it make a difference if the current governmental leaders prayed privately for God's wisdom?

4. What eventually happened to the Israelites?

5. According to Wiersbe, what is the first step toward revival and returning to the Lord? Practically, how would we know or see progress in this area?

6. Wiersbe notes that even if only a few seek the Lord, it makes a difference. How might this change your attitude toward revival?

7. In this passage, what does it mean to seek the Lord? What does it NOT mean? Why should we seek the Lord?

8. What is your reaction to Wiersbe's statement, "If we don't change our ways He may take our lives"? (See Acts 5:1-11; 1 Cor. 11:26-30.)

9. What is the proper role of human government? How can the church find the proper balance in political/societal involvement? (See Rom. 13:1-7; 1 Peter 2:13-17; Acts 4:18-20; 5:27-42).

10. What have you taken a stand against? What effect do you think you could have by speaking up?

Optional Activities
1. Set aside a special time to prayerfully consider the challenges from the end of the chapter: (a) Hear God's Word! (Am I listening?) (b) Seek the Lord! (Am I praying?) and (c) Seek the good! (Do I hate that which is evil?)

2. Meditate on the following verses and choose one to memorize. Psalm 63:1; Proverbs 8:17; Isaiah 55:6; Matthew 6:33; Luke 11:10.

Prayer Focus
Thank God for His mercy in that He lets us seek Him and find Him. Ask God to keep you daily returning and seeking Him with all your heart.

Assignment
1. Read Amos 5:18–6:14.

2. Read chapter 5 of *Be Concerned*, and look over the study guide.

Chapter Five

"Woe to the Sinners!"
(Amos 5:18-6:14)

Session Topic
Amos pronounced woe upon the ignorant, indifferent, indulgent, and impudent people of the nation of Israel.

Community Builders
1. When you envision the "day of doom" with no hiding places, what do you imagine and how do you feel?

2. Read aloud 1 Corinthians 10:6-12. Discuss why it is so difficult to learn from history.

Group Discussion Questions
1. What are the definitions of ignorant, indifferent, indulgent, and impudent?

2. If someone were to ask you, "What is the Day of the Lord?" how would you answer?

3. Wiersbe states, "Good theology can lead to hope, but bad theology leads to false hopes." What is an example of each?

4. In concern for others, what fruit do you see local churches bearing? (Read James 1:27; 2:8, 14-17.)

5. In what way, if any, can our country claim the same promises God made to Israel? (See Deut. 7:12-21; 2 Chron. 7:14.)

6. Although we may not worship actual idols, we do struggle with complacency in our worship. What is Wiersbe's definition of complacency? How does this compare with our concept of a lukewarm Christian?

7. What is the relationship between spiritual disciplines and indulgence?

8. How might our relatively indulgent lifestyles and exploitation of the poor be related? Give a specific example.

9. Wiersbe says that it is OK to enjoy good food and music as long as "the things of the Lord are uppermost in your heart." How can a person be confident of what is in his own heart?

10. What are some signs that a person is a lover of pleasure instead of a lover of God?

11. In what area of life do you suspect you have become accustomed to the dark?

Optional Activities

1. Watch and listen this week for examples of theologies that lead to hope or false hope.

2. Interview someone who practices spiritual disciplines. Find out if and how this has affected their love of pleasure.

Prayer Focus

Praise God for His care for the poor and oppressed. Ask God that He mold you into a lover of God instead of a lover of pleasure.

Assignment

1. Read Amos 7:1–9:15.

2. Read chapter 6 of *Be Concerned*, and look over the study guide.

Chapter Six

Stop—Look—Listen!
(Amos 7:1–9:15)

Session Topic

Amos is given special visions which center around his struggle with God and men, his declaration that judgment is coming, and the affirmation that God is working out His perfect plan.

Community Builders

1. Discuss the relationship between God's sovereignty and world history. Does God control every event?

2. Amos' trouble with religious leaders was nothing new. Review Acts 4:1-31. What observations can you make regarding Peter and John's situation? How might you apply these lessons today?

Group Discussion Questions

1. How do you understand the phrase, "The Lord changed His mind?" (7:2-6) See also Jeremiah 15:6; 18:1-10; Psalm 106:40-46.

2. What is the meaning of the plumb line? (Amos 7:8)

3. What was the purpose of proclaiming the impending destruction of Israel? Wasn't it already too late?

4. Jeroboam wanted to silence Amos. What difficult messages from the Lord in the Bible do you sometimes feel like silencing?

5. Why were both prophets and priests needed in the land at the time? In what way, if any, are these roles found in the church today?

6. What was the significance of the basket of fruit? (8:2)

7. What were some of the ways the Israelites did NOT

love their neighbors?

8. As you read Amos 8:11-13, what struck you the most? When have you thirsted for the word of the Lord?

9. What are the four affirmations from the heart of the Lord as categorized by Wiersbe?

10. What is the hope of 9:8-10? What important reminder does this give us as we ponder the terrible judgment God poured out on the Israelites?

Optional Activities

1. Summarize in your own words the sins of Israel and Judah, and the message of Amos to them. Write in a sentence what you have learned about God from studying the Book of Amos.

2. Read again how Amos prayed in chapter 7. Try to recall or find the prayers of other prophets. How can this challenge your praying?

Prayer Focus

Praise God that He hears our prayers and has compassion toward people with humble, repentant hearts and lives. Ask that your heart and life would be purified through the Holy Spirit and become more and more pleasing in His sight.

Assignment

1. Read Obadiah.

2. Read chapter 7 of *Be Concerned,* and look over the study guide.

Chapter Seven

A Tale of Two Brothers
(Obadiah 1-21)

Session Topic
Obadiah had a vision that denounced Edom's arrogance and feuding with Israel, pronounced coming judgment, and announced the future secure kingdom of Jacob.

Community Builders
1. How can we interpret world events today and know which are as God wants them to be? How does democracy and working for change fit in with God's sovereignty?

2. Which questions about God's sovereignty trouble you the most? What about God's sovereignty gives you the most comfort?

Group Discussion Questions
1. What is at the root of bitter feuds? What is so powerful that the participants don't even desire an end to the feud?

2. What is the worst example of a feud that you know of?

3. What is the answer to a long-standing, bitter feud? How might this affect U.S. foreign policy?

4. Was it a sin, or part of God's plan, for Jacob to steal Esau's blessing? Discuss Romans 8:28 in this regard.

5. After Jacob and Esau's great reconciliation in Genesis 32, what went wrong? (See Ezek. 32.)

6. What was the purpose of Obadiah's vision?

7. How do you see God's sovereignty at work in the world? What can we do to cooperate with His plans?

8. Why does God especially hate prideful arrogance in people and nations?

9. What judgment did God proclaim He would send to

the nation of Edom? For which sins was God going to judge Edom?

10. When has application of the Golden Rule changed your behavior?

11. What can we hope for in the future? How can we nurture this hope and keep it fresh and alive?

Optional Activities
1. Meditate on and memorize Obadiah 15; Matthew 7:12; and Galatians 6:9.

2. Do a biblical word study on the present and future kingdom of God.

Prayer Focus
Praise God that He is just in all His dealings with people and nations. Ask that He ignite a burning desire within you to reach out to the lost with the Gospel.

Assignment
1. Read Micah, especially chapters 1–2.

2. Read chapter 8 of *Be Concerned*, and look over the study guide.

C h a p t e r   E i g h t

Judgment Is Coming!
(Micah 1–2)

Session Topic
Micah saw the coming judgment and called the Jews to return to faithful worship and righteous living, but to no avail.

Community Builders
1. Materialism (or covetousness) is a topic often denounced by the prophets. What specific steps can we, as believers in this wealthy country, take to guard against this sin?

2. As Micah contemplated the judgment coming to Israel, he began to weep, wail, howl, and moan. How does the thought of judgment coming to the unsaved affect you? Why are we often so matter-of-fact about it?

Group Discussion Questions
1. What are the three messages that the Lord gave to Micah to deliver to the Israelites? (See chapter outline of Micah.)

2. If you picture the opening passage of Micah as a court-room (as does Wiersbe), how is it alike and how is it different than a contemporary courtroom?

3. Why was Micah so sad that he said he must "lament and wail"?

4. What does the phrase "her wound is incurable" point to?

5. As Wiersbe asks, how could the Lord Jehovah permit such suffering and shame to come to His covenant people?

6. In what way did covetousness especially show up with the Israelites? What are the definitions of "covetousness" and "materialism"?

7. What was the shallow theology the false prophets of

Israel espoused at this time?

8. Why did Micah's message contain both conviction and hope? What would one without the other communicate?

9. Of conviction and hope, which one would you be most prone to leave out when communicating the Gospel message? Why?

10. What in your church or your own spiritual life are you concerned may be "soft religion" that pampers your pride and makes it easy to sin?

Optional Activities

1. Read 2 Timothy 3:12. If you are not being persecuted, what does this mean about your spiritual life? What exceptions might there be to this principle?

2. Using the verses supplied by Wiersbe at the end of the chapter, study to learn more about the "remnant." Who are they? Why are they important? What is their destiny?

Prayer Focus

Praise the Lord for the conviction of sin given by the Holy Spirit and for the hope we have in Christ. Ask God for wisdom and strength to withstand the temptation of covetousness.

Assignment

1. Read Micah 3–5.

2. Read chapter 9 of *Be Concerned*, and look over the study guide.

Chapter Nine

A Ruler Is Coming!
(Micah 3-5)

Session Topic
Micah rebuked the leaders of Israel for their sinful conduct, spoke of their coming judgment, and also prophesied of the glorious future planned for them.

Community Builders
1. When you have something very important to say, how do you let others know when you want their full attention? In a letter, what words would you use to grab the reader's attention? Give specific examples.

2. The Israelite leaders turned a deaf ear to the Word of the Lord. When have you, even temporarily, turned a deaf ear to God's Word? How did it turn out? If you know someone who is doing this, what might you do to encourage a turnaround?

Group Discussion Questions
1. Consider the calls to attention such as Jesus gave, "He who has ears, let him hear" (Matt. 11:15). See also Hebrews 3:7-8; Proverbs 7:24. Compare these with James 1:22-25. How can you tell when someone is truly listening?

2. Give a description of people who hate the evil and do the good. What are they like?

3. Why do you think the word of the Lord through Micah contained such a vicious image of the rulers? (3:1-3)

4. What people might be functioning as false prophets today, "Whose lies made it easy for the corrupt officials to carry on their evil deeds" (Wiersbe)?

5. How can we balance being lovingly sensitive to people

but not trying too much to please them?

6. The Jews had false confidence because of their incorrect understanding of God and His promises. What false confidence toward God have you heard people proclaim?

7. Titus 1:16 describes people who "profess that they know God, but in works they deny Him." How would you confront a person like this? In what area of your life is this empty professing evident?

8. Wiersbe says, "When the outlook is grim, try the uplook." When things in your life look grim, how does "looking up" help you? What means does God provide for a Christian who needs renewal?

9. In your explanation of the Gospel to an unbeliever, how does the subject of heaven enter in? If someone were to grasp the significance of this hope of heaven, what would you expect to occur?

10. What does this statement of Wiersbe's mean to you: "Future hope ought to produce present holiness"?

Optional Activities
1. If you were to speak to Christian leaders today, what topic and biblical texts would you choose?

2. Meditate on your future hope in Christ. See Revelation 21; 1 Corinthians 15:35-58; Ephesians 1; especially verses 18-21.

Prayer Focus
Thank God for the strong and obedient role model of Micah. Pray that you may, like him, be "filled with power—with the Spirit of the Lord—and with justice and courage" (3:8).

Assignment
1. Read Micah 6–7.

2. Read chapter 10 of *Be Concerned*, and look over the study guide.

Chapter Ten
"Thy Kingdom Come"
(Micah 6-7)

Session Topic
Micah's third and last message was that the Israelites were guilty before the Lord and would be punished; however, God graciously promised mercy in the future.

Community Builders
1. If your group is familiar with it, sing the praise song based on Micah 6:8, "He Has Shown Thee."

2. What issues of justice are important for you? Why do we often bypass opportunities to do acts of justice and kindness? In what ways would this group serve someone in need?

Group Discussion Questions
1. Why was it so important that Israel obey the Lord?

2. Wiersbe's paraphrase of Micah's closing message is "Trust the Lord, not in spite of these things but *because of these things!*" What does this mean?

3. For what sins did the Israelites have great guilt? What was God's justification for their coming punishment?

4. At what times are there probably spiritual battles going on of which we are unaware, and yet God is protecting us? What thanks do we give Him?

5. Why is the word "remember" so important in our spiritual life?

6. When people try to justify themselves by their own works, what are they ignorant of?

7. What negative results occur when a person tries to "do penance" without truly repenting and trusting God's mercy?

8. Micah 6:8 does not mention belief or faith as a requirement of God. How can you fit this together with John 6:28–29?

9. What does it mean that people "reap what they sow"? When might there be, or seem to be, exceptions to this truism?

10. What caused distrust and disintegration within the Israelites' families?

11. When the future seems hopeless, how can our trust in God be strengthened?

Optional Activities

1. Memorize and study carefully Micah 6:8. Determine what each part means and make one practical application for yourself from the three requirements.

2. Read aloud Micah 7:18-19 as a prayer of praise. If you are musical, make it into a song.

Prayer Focus

Praise the Lord for His incredible compassion toward us. Pray that you can live out doing justly, loving mercy and kindness, and walking humbly with your God.

Assignment

1. Read Zephaniah, especially 1:1–2:15.

2. Read chapter 11 of *Be Concerned*, and look over the study guide.

C h a p t e r   E l e v e n

There's a Great Day Coming!
(Z e p h a n i a h   1 : 1 – 2 : 1 5)

Session Topic
Zephaniah exhorts the Jews that the terrible Day of the Lord is coming, and he urges them to repent of their sins and turn to the Lord for His forgiveness.

Community Builders
1. What hymns or praise songs can you think of with warnings of coming judgment? (You may want to look through hymnals or song booklets.) Why do you think there are so few? Why do we often neglect the teaching of, or even thoughts of, God's anger, indignation, fury, jealousy, wrath, and vengeance?

2. Read the key verses of 1:14 and 2:3 aloud. Share any observations you have on these verses.

Group Discussion Questions
1. The name Zephaniah means "Jehovah hides" or "Jehovah protects." What comfort does this give you? What mental picture do you have of this hiding place or protection?

2. What is our responsibility toward others concerning the Day of the Lord? What should we say? In what settings should we say it?

3. How would you interpret 1:2-3? What support do you have for this interpretation? What are the problems for this interpretation?

4. If God were to clear out the idols in our culture today, what would they be and what might He do?

5. What are the different groups of people God announced that He would "cut off"? (1:4-6)

171

6. Which specific sins does Zephaniah announce judgment for?

7. What does Zephaniah plead in response to the foretelling of awful judgment to come?

8. Who is left after the judgments are done? How did they survive?

9. Why can God hold the Gentile nations responsible when they never had the Law? What happened to these Gentile nations?

10. How can we be in the world but not be conformed to the world? What or who is "the world"? How do we wrongly imitate their ways?

11. What do you believe about the current application of the promise that "those who bless Israel, God will bless; those who curse Israel, God will curse"?

Optional Activities

1. How would you describe the people Zephaniah calls "stagnant in spirit"? (NASB) Look at different translations of 1:12. See also Revelation 3:15-16.

2. List the words in Zephaniah 1:14-18 which describe how terrible the Day of the Lord will be for the unrepentant. For further reading, see Revelation 6–19.

Prayer Focus

Thank God that He promises to protect the people who turn to Him. Pray that He would keep you from becoming complacent or stagnant in your faith.

Assignment

1. Read Zephaniah 3:1-20.

2. Read chapter 12 of *Be Concerned*, and look over the study guide.

C h a p t e r   T w e l v e

The Glory of the Kingdom
(Zephaniah 3:1-20)

Session Topic
Even though God's judgment is coming in the Day of the Lord, there is a great hope for both Gentiles and Jews.

Community Builders
1. If you felt led to write a letter to a Christian friend who was living a sinful lifestyle, what would you put at the beginning, middle, and end of the letter?

2. As a parent who loves your child, how do you or will you deal with deliberate disobedience? What if this disobedience is repeated over and over? How is this the same and different than God's dealings with His children?

Group Discussion Questions
1. Why do you think prophets always end their messages with words of hope?

2. How would you describe Jerusalem during Zephaniah's time?

3. The people and leaders of Israel continued in their flagrantly sinful lifestyle and were not heeding God's words and correction. What crucial part of God's covenant with them were they forgetting?

4. What hope for the future could the Gentiles look forward to? Does this include all Gentiles?

5. Wiersbe writes that after the Day of the Lord is over, a believing remnant will be left. What will have happened to the rest of Israel?

6. During the "kingdom" time, what will the lives of the remnant be like?

7. According to Wiersbe, what will be the purpose of feasts and sacrifices in the future kingdom?

8. What lesson can we learn from someone who has strayed from God's will?

9. What are some current examples of the consequences of forgiven sin?

10. What significance do you see in the description of God's motherly qualities? (3:17)

Optional Activities
1. What prevented the Israelites from hearing and heeding God's word? Prayerfully examine yourself for any similarities. (See Ps. 139:23–24.)

2. Read the passages on the "motherhood of God" as listed in note 4. Imagine receiving this nurturing from God. In what way does that seem different from the more common fatherly images?

Prayer Focus
Praise God for His faithfulness to bless, chasten, and forgive. Ask God to help you not be stiff-necked but to have a humble and contrite spirit before Him.

Assignment
1. Read chapter 13 of *Be Concerned*, and look over the study guide.

Chapter Thirteen

The Company of the Concerned

Session Topic
Be concerned about the condition of your nation and its leaders, working with others in the "company of the concerned" to make a difference for God's kingdom.

Community Builders
1. Discuss what grieves you the most about your nation today.

2. What role can you and your "company of the concerned" fulfill in God's work? Create a group motto that would be an inspiration to that end.

Group Discussion Questions
1. How would you define the "company of the concerned"?

2. Who do you know, if anyone, who truly grieves and laments over sin?

3. What is anguish? When have you felt this? Why don't we feel it more often?

4. In what way were the true prophets good examples for us to follow?

5. What is your opinion on the place of formal training for ministry?

6. What negative and positive results have come for the Gospel because the U.S.A. is known as a "Christian nation"? How would you describe the U.S.A. in this regard?

7. What can we learn from Nehemiah's response when he heard about the tragic condition of Jerusalem? (Neh. 1–2)

8. Where do you see similarities and differences between the Jewish nation's relationship with God and the U.S.A. and

its relationship to God?

9. According to Wiersbe, what should be expected from leaders in a democracy? Would you add anything?

10. How can you promote righteousness in your current life circumstances?

Optional Activities

1. Gather a group of like-minded believers to be a "company of the concerned." Set goals, even if it is a short-term group. Pray for God's direction in your fellowship and your plans.

2. Write out an answer to the question, "How would you describe the books of the Minor Prophets to someone not familiar with the Bible?" (If you answered this question for Community Builder 1 from chapter 1, compare your two answers.) You could also make a timeline of the prophets and concurrent historical events.

Prayer Focus

Praise the Lord that He has always preserved a remnant to carry on His work. Ask the Lord to work in your heart so you can feel anguish over sin and to enable you to take action with a "company of the concerned."

N O T E S

Chapter 1

1. "The Deserted Village" by Oliver Goldsmith, lines 51 and 52.

2. How could Amos rightfully announce judgment to the Gentile nations that had never been given the Law of God? On the basis of natural law and conscience (Rom. 1:18–2:16). When humans brutally sin against each other, they sin against God; for humans are made in the image of God. When Amos denounced the Jews, he appealed to the Law of God as well (Amos 2:4).

3. See *Miracle at Philadelphia* by Catherine Drinker Bowen (Boston: Little, Brown, 1966), p. 126. While there is no evidence that Franklin was an evangelical Christian, he was indeed a God-fearing man.

4. Amos did not mention Gath because by that time it had lost its prominence and had been subjected to Jewish authority (2 Chron. 26:6; see also Zeph. 2:4-5; Zech. 9:5-6).

5. Though the statement is anonymous, it is usually attributed to the German author Friedrich von Logau whose writings were translated into English by Henry Wadsworth Longfellow. Von Logau found it quoted in a book by the second-century Greek philosopher Sextus Empiricus.

6. Shakespeare had inscribed on his gravestone:

> Good friend, for Jesu's sake forbear
> To dig the dust enclosed here.
> Blest be the man that spares these stones,
> And curst be he that moves my bones.

7. "Kerioth" (Amos 2:2) can also be translated "of her cities" (NIV margin), but it's likely Kerioth is the name of a Moabite city, possibly the capital city of the nation. Kerioth of Moab is mentioned in Jeremiah 48:24 and 41. There was also a Kerioth in Judah (Josh. 15:25), and it's possible that Judas Iscariot ("ish Kerioth = man of Kerioth") came from there.

8. Under the Mosaic Covenant, God promised to bless His people if they obeyed His Law but to remove His blessing if they disobeyed (Deut. 27–29). However, the people forgot that God often blessed them in spite of their sins so that He might be faithful to

His promises to Abraham and David. In His love and long-suffering, God sent them messengers to call them back to obedience; but they refused to listen. "Because sentence against an evil work is not executed speedily, therefore the heart of the sons of men is fully set in them to do evil" (Ecc. 8:11).

Chapter 2

1. Note in Numbers 10 that trumpets were used to warn the people of danger, especially impending invasion.

Chapter 3

1. "Keeping Up with the Joneses" was the name of a popular newspaper comic strip that ran for twenty-eight years. It told the story of a man of limited means, who tried to keep up with his neighbors.

2. Bashan was a fertile area east of the Sea of Galilee in the tribe of Manasseh and was known for its fine livestock (Deut. 32:14; Ps. 22:12; Ezek. 39:18).

3. The end of verse 3 presents a problem. The KJV translates it "shall cast them into the palace," while the NIV, NKJV and NASB read "cast out toward [or into] Harmon." Amos uses the Hebrew word twelve times; it's translated "palaces" in the KJV, and except for Amos 4:3, the NIV translates it "fortresses." The NIV text note gives "O mountain of oppression." If "Harmon" is a place, we don't know where it is. In his excellent commentary on Amos, Jeffrey Niehaus translates the sentence "and you will let go dominion" (*An Exegetical and Expository Commentary: The Minor Prophets*, edited by Thomas E. McComiskey [Grand Rapids: Baker Book House, 1992], vol. 1, 391). These women who were accustomed to giving orders would find themselves taking orders!

4. Both the NASB and the NIV translate the Hebrew word "the last of you," meaning "nobody will escape," but the KJV and NKJV translate it "posterity." However, the NIV translates the same word as "descendants" in 1 Kings 21:21, Psalm 109:13, and Daniel 11:4.

5. The word "irony" comes from a Greek word (*eironeia*), which means "to speak deceptively, with dissimulation." What you say is to be interpreted just the opposite of what the words convey. (For

other examples in Scripture, see Jud. 10:4; Ezek. 10:39; 28:3).

6. Along with their annual tithes, the Jews were commanded to bring a special tithe every three years (Deut. 14:28; 26:12). The NIV renders it "every three years," but the Hebrew text reads "every three days" (NKJV; NASB) or "on the third day" (NIV margin), that is, "by the third day after you come to the sanctuary." It appears that Amos is again using "holy irony." "You are commanded to bring the special tithe every three years; but you are so spiritual, you bring tithes every three days!"

Chapter 4

1. "Virgin daughter of Israel" is a common phrase in the Old Testament (2 Kings 19:21; Isa. 37:22; Jer. 18:13; 31:4, 21; Lam. 2:13) and it is also applied to other nations, such as Egypt (Jer. 46:11) and Babylon (Isa. 47:1). It refers to an unmarried daughter still under the protection of the father. Because the nation of Israel turned their back on their Heavenly Father, they got into trouble and were defiled and slain in their own land. Paul used a similar image in writing about the local church (2 Cor. 11:1-3).

2. The Jews associated Beersheba with God's appearing to Abraham (Gen. 21:31-33), Isaac (26:23-25), and Jacob (46:1-5).

3. J.B. Phillips, *Four Prophets: A Translation into Modern English* (New York: The Macmillan Co., 1963), 14.

4. The Hebrew word *mishpat* is translated "justice" in most modern translations and usually "judgment" in the KJV. The NIV uses "justice" in Amos 2:7; 5:7, 12, 15, 24; 6:12. The root word of *mishpat* is *shapat*, which means "to govern." The aim of government is justice for all people. The prophet Isaiah also pleaded for justice in the land.

Chapter 5

1. Amos 5:26 is a difficult verse to translate and interpret. Is it referring to Israel past or the nation during Amos' day, or both? Ezekiel 20:5-9 makes it clear that Israel learned idolatry in Egypt and ignored the fact that the plagues God sent were a judgment against these false gods (Ex. 12:12). Ezekiel 20:10-17 informs us that the Jewish people also practiced idolatry in the wilderness. The point Amos makes is that the people didn't learn from their

past, a problem the church has today. "What experience and history teach is this," wrote G.W. Hegel, "that nations and governments have never learned anything from history, or acted upon any lessons they might have drawn from it."

2. The Hebrew phrase translated "chief ointments" parallels Exodus 30:23, where the formula for the sacred anointing oil is given. Perhaps the careless Israelites were duplicating the holy oil for their own private use. If so, then we have an even greater sin—using the holy things of God for their own personal pleasure.

3. The phrase is used in Amos 8:7 to refer to God Himself, but that can't be the meaning here. The Jews prided themselves that their God was the true and living God, even though they often indulged in the worship of idols. They were also proud of the temple in Jerusalem (Ezek. 24:21). They might have been proud of God, but God certainly wasn't proud of them!

4. Some versions translate verse 12 "or plow the sea with oxen." However, to do so requires a slight change in the Hebrew text.

Chapter 6

1. The Bible often uses human concepts to describe divine actions or emotions, such as God resting (Gen. 2:2), grieving (6:6), clapping His hands (Ezek. 21:17), laughing (Ps. 2:4), and writing (Ex. 31:18). When God "relents" ("repents" KJV), it doesn't mean that He made a mistake and has to change His mind. Rather, it means that He maintains His intentions but changes His way of working. A good illustration is found in Jeremiah 18:1-17.

2. Of course, the temple was in Jerusalem, but Amos is referring to the places of worship in Israel, such as the king's chapel. Since the word translated "temple" can also be translated "palace" (2 Kings 20:18), the prophet may have been referring to the banquets of the king.

3. A.W. Tozer, *The Knowledge of the Holy* (New York: Harper & Brothers, 1961), 11.

4. James quoted Amos 9:11 during the Jerusalem conference when the leaders discussed the matter of the place of the Gentiles in the church (Acts 15). The question was, "Must a Gentile become a Jew in order to become a Christian?" But note that James did not

say that Amos 9:11 was *fulfilled* by the Gentiles' coming into the church, but that the prophets (plural) *agreed with* the Gentiles' being a part of the church (Acts 15:13-18). After all, if believing Gentiles are one day going to be a part of the Messianic Kingdom (David's dynasty restored), why can't they be a part of the church today? Why should they be forced to become Jewish proselytes in order to become Christians? However, some interpret Amos 9:11 and the words of James to mean that the church is the "tabernacle of David" so that the Old Testament prophecies about the kingdom are now fulfilled in the church. How the church is like David's kingdom "as in the days of old" is difficult to understand, and the references to Edom (Amos 9:12) and the fruitfulness of the land (vv. 13-15) are also difficult to apply to the church.

Chapter 7

1. Edom and the Edomites are found over one hundred times in the Old Testament. They are mentioned in the prophecies of Isaiah (chap. 34), Jeremiah (chap. 49; Lam. 4:21-22), Ezekiel (25:12-14; 35:1-15), Daniel (11:41), Joel (3:19), Amos (1:6-11; 2:1; 9:12) and Malachi (1:4), as well as Obadiah. King Saul overcame them (1 Sam. 14:47), and so did David (2 Sam. 8:13-14; 1 Kings 11:14-16), but Edom was a thorn in Israel's side for centuries. Consult a map of Bible lands for the location of Edom.

2. Compare Obadiah 1-6 with Jeremiah 49:7-22. The prophets often quoted from one another.

3. The Prophet Joel has a great deal to say about "the Day of the Lord." See my book *Be Amazed*, which expounds Joel's prophecy.

Chapter 8

1. For other pictures of God coming like a warrior, see Exodus 15, Psalm 18, Isaiah 63, and Habakkuk 3.

2. The Prophet Hosea used the image of adultery to describe the sin of the nation in worshiping idols. In fact, Hosea's own wife was guilty of adultery and prostitution, and he had to buy her out of the slave market! See my book *Be Amazed* for an exposition of the Book of Hosea (Victor Books).

3. Several of these towns were located within a nine-mile radius

of Micah's hometown, Moresheth Gath, and could easily be seen from there on a clear day. These were Micah's neighbors, and he had to tell them they were doomed to destruction!

4. How Lachish was "the beginning of sin" to Judah is not explained. Lachish was the most important and most powerful city-state in the Shephelah, and the Assyrians were very proud that they had conquered it. It was a highly fortified city, and the confidence of the people of Lachish and of Judah was in their military might, not in the Lord. This pride and self-assurance was the beginning of the nation's sin. The leaders depended on the outlying fortress cities to keep the enemy from invading, but these cities fell to the enemy.

5. See Isaiah 1:9; 7:3; 10:20-22; 11:11, 16; Jeremiah 6:9; 23:3; 31:7; 40:11; Ezekiel 11:13; 14:22; Zephaniah 2:4-9; Haggai 1:12, 14; and Zechariah 8:1-8. Micah writes of the remnant in 2:12, 4:7, 5:3, 5:7-8, and 7:18. Paul uses the doctrine of the remnant to prove that God has not forsaken the Jewish people in this present age (Rom. 9; see also 11:1-6).

Chapter 9

1. This statement is found eight times in the Bible (Lev. 11:44-45; 19:2; 20:7, 26; 21:8, 15; 1 Peter 1:15-16).

2. The traditional verse division at 5:4-5 is unfortunate. "And this man shall be the peace" (or "their peace") belongs at the end of verse 4, not at the beginning of verse 5. The reference is to Jesus Christ the Messiah.

3. Isaiah painted the same picture (2:1-4). Some interpret these passages in a spiritual sense as describing the church today, but, I prefer to see them as specific prophecies for the Jewish nation. The conditions on earth described by Isaiah and Micah haven't appeared, especially the elimination of war, anti-Semitism, and religious rivalry among nations.

4. Does the "exaltation" of Jerusalem (v. 1) mean only that it will be honored and distinguished by the Lord, or that there will be actual changes in the topography of the land? The latter seems to be the case. The NIV translates verse 1, "It will be raised above the hills," which suggests the literal raising of Mt. Zion to a place of

special prominence. Zechariah 14:4-5 indicates that there will be changes in the topography when Christ returns.

5. Contrast with Joel 3:10, where the opposite picture is described.

6. It is unwise to make Micah 5:1 a prophecy of what happened to Jesus during His trial, although He was slapped in the face, beaten with a reed, and scourged (Matt. 27:30; Mark 15:19; John 19:3). The context of Micah 5:1 is definitely the siege of Jerusalem, not the trial of Jesus.

Chapter 10

1. However, Micah 6:8 must not be mistaken as a condemnation of the Mosaic sacrificial system. It was right for the Jews to bring their sacrifices to God *if their hearts had been broken in repentance and confession of sin.* God wants obedience, not sacrifice (1 Sam. 15:22), and the most important sacrifice is that of a broken and contrite heart (Ps. 51:16). See also Isaiah 1:11-15 and Hosea 6:6. Worship that doesn't produce a godly life is not true worship at all.

2. The phrase "hear ye the rod" (KJV) or "Heed the rod" (NIV) is a puzzle to translators and expositors. What or who is "the rod"? Does it refer to the punishment God sent to the nation or to the nation that brought the punishment? Or does it refer to the Lord Himself? According to Isaiah 10:5, God calls Assyria "the rod of My anger." In *The Minor Prophets: An Exegetical and Expository Commentary,* Dr. Bruce Waltke suggests an alternate translation: "Give heed, O tribe, and the assembly of the city" (Grand Rapids: Baker Book House), vol. 2, p. 736. When the officials met in assembly to consider business, each tribal leader would have his official staff symbolizing his authority (see Num. 17). God addresses not only the city of Jerusalem in general but also specifically the leaders who met to consider what to do.

3. We must be careful not to develop an "Elijah complex" and think we're the only godly people left (1 Kings 19:10). David felt that way (Ps. 12:1, and so did Isaiah (57:1). But in Micah's case, the godly remnant was so small that it seemed insignificant.

4. Micah 7:8-10 certainly expresses the feelings and hopes of the exiles from both Israel and Judah. Eventually both Assyria and Babylon were defeated and passed off the scene, but it wasn't the

Jews who conquered them. The Jews' return from Babylonian exile was a small picture of the greater regathering of Israel that will take place in the last days (Isa. 11:11-16; Matt. 24:31).

Chapter 11

1. Strictly speaking, any time of divine judgment could be called "the Day of the Lord." Local judgments were but examples of the final "Day of the Lord" to occur in the end times.

2. Some students call this "Josiah's revival," but it's doubtful that "revival" is the best word. Certainly the people put away their false gods and returned to the worship of Jehovah, but their motivation was not spiritual. Since the king commanded them to abandon the foreign gods, the people obeyed more from a fear of the king than a love for the Lord. The changes were only on the surface of the nation; the people's hearts were still devoted to the false gods. No sooner was Josiah dead than the nation reverted back to their old ways. What they experienced was a surface reformation but not a deep revival.

3. The hymn is attributed to Thomas of Celano. This translation of "Dies Irae" ("day of wrath") is by William J. Irons.

4. The root of the Hebrew word means either "black," referring to the color of their robes (Jewish priests wore white), or "zealous," referring to the frenzy of their religious ceremonies as they prostrated themselves before their gods.

5. For other instances of judgment depicted as sacrifice, see Isaiah 34:5-7, Jeremiah 46:10, and Ezekiel 39:17-19; and note Revelation 19:17-21.

6. The phrase "leap on [over] the threshold" in verse 9 is usually related to the pagan practice described in 1 Samuel 5:1-5, but perhaps it describes the haste with which the covetous Jews left their houses to go out to exploit the poor and acquire wealth to devote to their false gods. The prophets condemned the rich for their brutal treatment of the poor in the land.

7. *Maktesh* means "mortar" in Hebrew, possibly because the district lay in a part of Jerusalem that was in a natural depression. But perhaps there is a double meaning here: God would deal with His people the way women pound grain in a mortar.

8. The Hebrew word translated "jealousy" (1:18; 3:8) means "to be hot, to be inflamed." God's jealousy is not like human envy, for what could God envy when He has everything? He is jealous over His name and His glory, and His anger is aroused when His people worship other gods (Ex. 34:14; Pss. 78:58; 79:5). God is jealous over His people and wants their wholehearted love and devotion.

Chapter 12

1. See Nehemiah 11:1, 18; Isaiah 48:2; 52:1; Daniel 9:24; Matthew 4:5; 27:53; Revelation 11:2; 21:2; 22:19.

2. Interpreters are divided over whether the prophets are speaking literally (a real temple with real priests and sacrifices) or metaphorically (the temple as symbolic of worship and service in the new Kingdom Age). Certainly the prophets had to use language and images that the people understood, but if these predictions are not to be taken literally, it's difficult to understand why the prophets (especially Ezekiel) wrote in such great detail.

3. The Hebrew phrase has been variously explained: "He will quiet you with His love"; "He will be silent in His love" (i.e., not bring up your past sins); "He will renew you in His love"; "He will renew your love for Him"; "His love for you will make everything new." Perhaps it all means the same thing: A new and deeper relationship with God will bring peace and joy and make all things new.

4. Other passages that speak of the "motherhood of God" are Isaiah 49:14-16; 66:13 and Matthew 23:37-39. Psalm 131 might also be included, and see also 1 Thessalonians 2:7-8.

Chapter 13

1. Statistics taken from *The Index of Leading Cultural Indicators* by William J. Bennett (New York: Simon and Schuster, 1994).

2. This statement isn't a criticism of ministerial education. Since I teach for several evangelical Christian schools, I'm not anti-intellectual. But often God lays hold of "untrained" people and trains them in His own way to accomplish His work. There's a place in God's vineyard for a brilliant Jonathan Edwards and also for a D.L. Moody, who probably had the equivalent of a sixth-grade education.